Destined to Flourish

Tina Carpenter

DESTINED TO FLOURISH

Onwards and Upwards Publications, Berkeley House,
11 Nightingale Crescent, West Horsley, Surrey KT24 6PD

www.onwardsandupwards.org

copyright © Tina Carpenter 2014

The right of Tina Carpenter to be identified as the author of this work has been asserted by the author in accordance with the Copyright, Designs and Patents Act 1988.

All rights reserved.

No part of this publication may be reproduced or transmitted in any form or by any means, electronic or mechanical, including photocopy, recording or any information storage and retrieval system, without permission in writing from the author or publisher.

THE HOLY BIBLE, NEW INTERNATIONAL VERSION®, NIV® Copyright © 1973, 1978, 1984, 2011 by Biblica, Inc.® Used by permission. All rights reserved worldwide.

Scriptures and additional materials marked GNB are from the Good News Bible © 1994 published by the Bible Societies/HarperCollins Publishers Ltd UK, Good News Bible© American Bible Society 1966, 1971, 1976, 1992. Used with permission.

Scripture marked NKJV taken from the New King James Version®. Copyright © 1982 by Thomas Nelson, Inc. Used by permission. All rights reserved.

ISBN: 978-1-910197-04-2
Cover design: Leah-Maarit

Printed in the UK

Endorsements

It has been my joy and privilege to have been Tina's pastor for some fourteen years now. In this time I have seen her work through many challenges and come through many battles… and what has emerged is a woman of such wisdom and spiritual substance. I am so blessed to be able to endorse this book which I believe will be instrumental in helping so many enjoy inner restoration, healing and transformation.

God tells us in Jeremiah 29:11, "For I know the thoughts that I think toward you, says the Lord, thoughts of peace and not of evil, to give you a future and a hope" (NKJV). God does have a plan for your life, and it is a good plan. He has designed your life to be filled with purpose, destiny and prosperity. God loves you more than you will ever know… But there can be roadblocks to the fulfilment and abundance He desires you to have.

Tina's story is a powerful one of overcoming the roadblocks and the very things that the enemy of her faith attempted to use to derail her destiny and steal her future. It is an amazing testimony of the power of forgiveness and the importance of receiving God's forgiveness, forgiving ourselves and forgiving those who have hurt us.

Dr Brad Norman
Senior Pastor and Founder,
Salvation for the Nations International Churches

Tina Carpenter, through the medium of her own story of faith, conveys the love and grace of God in a straightforward and biblically informed way that may prove helpful to others seeking healing and redemption. That story is a moving testimony to the unfailing love of the God who meets us where we are and transforms us by his Spirit.

Rev'd Dr. Paul Goodliff
Ministries Team Leader,
Baptist Union of Great Britain

In this refreshingly honest and reflective biography, Tina takes us on a journey that allows God to peel off the layers of hurt, rejection, resentment and un-forgiveness, until our hearts are fully confronted with God's unrelenting heart and wholehearted commitment to remove everything that hinders His love for us and for others.

Tina successfully combines a reflective and witnessing approach, to expose God's commitment to restoring us to our God-given purpose. Ultimately she arrives at her conclusion, as a seeker of the truth – in a way that undoubtedly appeals to all ages, levels of maturity and people groups from every walk of life... A must read!

Mandi Tandi
Leader
Salvation for the Nations, UK

An honestly written and easy to read 'God Help' book covering many of the most common obstacles to knowing our Heavenly Father in the close and intimate way that He created us for. Each issue we might be dealing with stands on its own, which means the reader can dip in when seeking help for a specific area of need. The Bible verses are spot on for each section and there are suggestions for practical application. It is big on forgiveness and God's immense love, which are the keys to unlocking the chains that hold us captive.

Patricia Mingorance
Pastor
Christian Community International,
Almuñecar, Spain

…'Destined to Flourish' is an easy read which takes you through trails, disappointment, guilt and shame of family and relationships – personal or otherwise – [and] brings you to a new level of understanding [regarding] how to deal with difficult and emotional situations. [Tina shows] how that one person in her life was always there to bring her through.

This book has an anointing that speaks to you in ways you can never imagine.

Janet Chance
Film Producer
Herts International Church

When you pick up this book, you'll find it very hard to put down! It takes you on an emotive journey of a young girl growing up with all the odds stacked against her. The twists and turns in her young life leave a trail of devastation to the point where you can't imagine how any good can come out of it. The author cleverly weaves the secret keys she has learnt from an intimate walk with God that helped her to unlock those dark and damaged places, allowing the restoring grace of God's light and truth to dispel hopelessness, bit by bit.

It's a story of a journey to wholeness and a real desire to pass on the good news of living a life free from bitterness, dysfunction and isolation and turn it around to joy, fulfilment and the chance to dream again.

I would recommend this book to be used as an effective tool for anyone who has a heart to reach out in love to people who have lost their way in life.

Margaret Boonstra
Pastor
London International Church, Uxbridge

Acknowledgements

I thank my spiritual leaders who have not shied away from speaking and preaching the Truth in love, and particularly Paul Goodliff whose ministry, encouragement and counselling was pivotal in enabling me to find God in a more personal way.

I am eternally grateful to Kevin and Barbara Ashby, Robert, Katie and Chris, for their unconditional love, always accepting me just as I am and being for me the family I never had.

My teachers have been a significant part of my life, and without their encouragement and affirmation this book may never have been possible.

Thank you to all my wonderful friends, for the fun and laughter we've shared that has added an abundance of colour to my life. Particular thanks to Janet Chance, Kudzai Max and Tracey Muponda for the tremendous encouragement and support they've given as I've been writing this book.

Above all, I am and always will be grateful to the unfailing love of my Father God, the healing and restoring presence of His son Jesus Christ and the guidance, comfort and power of His Holy Spirit within me.

To God be the Glory.

About the Author

Tina is a mother of two and more recently a grandmother. She has had a career in nursing, obtaining a degree in Palliative Care and working several years in cancer care before moving into a non-clinical role. Now she runs her own business.

For many years, Tina served in a variety of ways within the church, including 'mums and toddlers' groups, leading Bible study and house groups, and actively participating in worship. Tina taught herself guitar to use in the house group setting and for many years played the flute, and later the saxophone in the church worship team and in local outreach events.

As Tina's desire to see people released from their problems and suffering grew, she was drawn more into pastoral care, studying for a diploma in Pastoral Counselling and using her experience and skills within the pastoral and healing ministries of her local church. In addition, she has served on the prayer ministry team at Soul Survivor summer camps, witnessing first hand miraculous healings and has also devoted time for nursing with Mercy Ships in West Africa.

Life doesn't stand still for Tina! In her thirties she enjoyed ice skating and obtained Gold medals in Ballroom and Latin American dancing; in her forties she learned tap dancing to intermediate level, finding the pleasure of performing on stage in dance shows. Now in her fifties, Tina has discovered Regiment Fitness – outdoor military style fitness training – and is proud to have completed a 10k military style obstacle race raising money for charity. Looking ahead, Tina has a desire to run the London marathon the year she is sixty and has a list of things to do when she retires, including teaching herself to play the keyboard, learning to play golf and water colour painting.

Tina believes life is for living; she often tells her friends, "It doesn't matter how many candles you have on your birthday cake; it's about how you feel inside the counts." Tina is committed to helping people receive physical and emotional healing, encouraging them to achieve freedom and fulfilment in their lives and to reach their God-given destiny.

If you wish to contact Tina, please write to:
tina@destinedtoflourish.com

This book is dedicated to
my son and daughter, Robin and Tania;
my grandchildren, Finley and Mia;
and the generations to come.

The obstacles I've overcome and
all that has been achieved in my life through Christ
has become your inheritance.

Contents

Foreword 13
Introduction 15
1. God Really Does Speak to Us! 17
2. Damaged Goods 24
3. Learning to Receive Love 34
4. Healing of Bad Memories 43
5. Forgive? Why Wouldn't I? 53
6. There's No Half Measure with God 64
7. Don't Believe Everything You Hear 72
8. We Can Move Mountains 80
9. False Accusations 86
10. The Dream Stealer 96
11. Reunited 103
12. Living in Freedom 112

www.destinedtoflourish.com

Foreword

I first met Tina thirty years ago when a mutual friend brought her along to a church house group that I was leading. Little did my wife and I realise that this would be the start of an ongoing friendship that would develop lasting bonds of love and respect as we grew to know more about each other and shared our stories and faith.

Tina had already started the journey she describes in this book, and we have had the privilege of accompanying her along some of the pathway she has subsequently walked. As we learned more about her past and background it became apparent that the grace of God was at work in her life and that she had a deep desire to explore and experience the depths of His love. We can testify to the fact that her journey has not been easy or without pain and sorrow, but through it all her faith has remained steadfast and God has continued the work in her that he started prior to our meeting.

Tina has a genuine desire to encourage and help those who are hurting, damaged and vulnerable, yet not with the simplistic solutions so often offered up in our world of quick fixes. Her offering is born from having worn the T-shirt and learned over time how to respond to God's grace and love. The transformations she describes are real and lasting; we are witnesses to that, and to the fact that she recognises that, like all of us, she is still a work in progress.

This book does not provide formulas for overcoming problems or struggles but rather shares the principles which Tina has learned to apply in her life, and she encourages the reader to follow her on the same journey. I have personally witnessed her transformation from a victim to an overcomer, and I thoroughly recommend her story to you.

Kevin Ashby
Elder, Langney Community Church
Eastbourne

Introduction

The Bible clearly states that when we become Christians we are a "new creation, the old has gone, the new has come" (2 Corinthians 5:17). Why is it then that Christians still suffer from depression, anxiety, low self-esteem and all the other emotional problems that anybody, whether Christian or not, can have? I believe the "new creation" relates to our spirit. Our minds and emotions still need transforming and healing, and this is an ongoing process.

I have sometimes wondered how I've got this far in life when I consider the circumstances and experiences of my early years. I grew up in an atmosphere of continual criticism and chronic deprivation of affection and affirmation. Some would suggest that a person damaged as I was in my early years could never achieve full potential in life and would be more likely to suffer from mental illness. I admit I've suffered at times from depression and low self-esteem, but there was always something inside me that kept me going. I have learned not to give in to anger, resentment or unforgiveness, but rather have chosen to embrace the ability to love and be loved and to experience a peace and contentment in my daily life whatever the circumstances. How can this be?

I believe this is only possible with God's grace, which is an expression of the love that God has for each of us, more than we could imagine, in spite of our failings, frustrations, insecurities, bitterness and lack of love for ourselves. His love seeks us out, encourages us and provides a way forward even when hope is fading. God's grace is for everyone, whether Christian or not, but not everyone recognises it, responds to it, or even knows how to respond.

God has designed each one of us with exactly what we require to overcome any and all of the difficult circumstances we experience in our early life. This sustains us until such time as we learn to recognise and receive God's unfailing love demonstrated through divine healing and restoration.

This book is written for everyone, whatever faith or belief, because God's love is for everyone. I share my story and the solutions I've discovered, which are based on Christian principles. I don't claim to have all the answers but I have found on my journey through life that there are certain common obstacles that we need to overcome in order to experience God's love in a deeper, fulfilling way. The order that these obstacles appear is not important; however, being able to recognise and overcome is what will develop in you an ability to become all that God has intended for you.

Chapter One

God Really Does Speak to Us!

It was a cold, snowy evening in December 1976, and I'd just finished carol singing around the hospital wards. I was a student nurse; I loved singing carols and a group of us nurses had had a great time that evening bringing festive joy to the patients and staff alike. Now I was cycling the seven miles to a friend's house, feeling the coolness of the frosty night air on my face and thinking how beautiful the stars were in the clear night sky.

Still running through my mind were the words of "Away in a Manger" and I started singing it aloud, over and over as I rode up and down the hills. The more I sang the words, the more it became a personal prayer: "Be near me Lord Jesus, I ask thee to stay close by me forever and love me I pray. Bless all the dear children in thy tender care, and fit us for heaven to live with thee there."

Suddenly the words seemed to come alive, and I couldn't help thinking of the children I'd just seen on the hospital ward. Some of them I knew well as

I'd recently finished my paediatric placement. One of the little girls was terminally ill with only days left to live and I started to feel angry. I stopped cycling, looked up to the sky and said aloud, "God, if you're real, show yourself to me." I waited. Nothing happened – no loud voices, no flashing lights – so I got back on my bike and rode on.

Now some people would wonder why I'd even thought of praying or talking to God; after all, I wasn't religious and didn't go to church. In fact I hadn't been brought up as a Christian at all, although in those days schools had Christian assemblies, so I did know the traditional hymns and I had been used to daily prayers at school. Not that I'd understood what I was singing or praying. My only memory of church was when my brother and I had stayed in foster care for six weeks before my parents divorced and the foster family had taken us to church each Sunday. All I remembered from those visits was a story about a little man called Zacchaeus who was up a tree – but I couldn't for the life of me remember what he was doing there or what happened next!

This night, out on my bike, was the second time in my life I'd prayed seriously. My first serious prayer had been when I was sixteen years old. Each night in desperation I would ask God to "take my mother", to make her die – and each morning I awoke to the sound of her voice and knew that my prayer hadn't been answered and that my nightmare life continued.

I say 'nightmare life' because I grew up in an extremely destructive and negative family atmosphere. My mother, who'd never learned how to express love, was continually making demands on me to the point that by the time I was doing my O-levels at school I could no longer concentrate on my homework in the evenings as she kept interrupting me, either to criticise or with tasks to do. I started to wake up in the early hours each night, unable to sleep, so decided that if I couldn't sleep then this was a good time to study without interruptions. This worked well for a short time until one night my mother noticed my bedroom light on. She aggressively entered my room and shouted at me, complaining that I was wasting her electricity. There were no questions or consideration from her about what I was doing and why I was awake. The next day on my way home from school I bought some candles and matches, and from then on I wrote all my essays during the night by candlelight without being noticed or interrupted.

Because God didn't reveal himself to me on that cold night in 1976, I continued to believe he couldn't be real. However, two years after that evening of carol singing in the hospital, a strange thing happened. It was the afternoon of 15th January, 1979, and I was in the maternity hospital having given birth to my first baby earlier that day.

Visiting time hadn't started and I was alone in the side room with my daughter, just watching her through the Perspex sides of the cot and thinking how amazingly beautiful she was. All of a sudden I felt another presence with me in the room. I couldn't see anything but I instinctively knew it was God and felt very calm and not at all frightened. God said into my spirit, "I have given you this baby; it's not what you have done, but it is a gift from me."

Now I know that all new babies are a miraculous sight, and this was not the first time I'd seen a new baby, having completed obstetrics training as a nurse, but at that moment something inside me changed; I was so grateful to God for this gift and had a thirst like never before for learning about Him. I remembered the cold, snowy night when I had asked God to show himself to me, and I knew now that God had answered my prayer: he had revealed himself to me and in addition given us the gift of a beautiful baby.

The next day there was a Christian service on the ward with Holy Communion. I'd no idea what it all meant but I knew I had to be there and take part. I started reading my Bible, the only one I had that I'd been given all those years ago when we were in foster care. It was the King James Version and although I'd looked at it many years earlier, I hadn't read it as it hadn't made sense to me, and quite honestly I'd found it boring. Now I was eagerly reading it, and it was starting to make sense! This was the beginning of my Christian life, the most amazing journey I've ever encountered. I didn't know then what being a Christian was all about but that didn't matter; I knew God's voice and His leading, and that has always sustained me.

I'm glad I became a Christian by God revealing himself this way, through His creation. Contrary to what many people think, Christianity is not about a set of rules or steps to follow; it's about knowing God and having a relationship with Him.

In the Garden of Eden, Adam and Eve knew God; indeed the Bible says God walked in the garden with them and they related closely to Him until they chose to listen to the voice of a serpent, the devil, and wilfully disobey God by eating the fruit from the tree of the knowledge of good and evil. This action had consequences not just for them but for everyone since. It brought sickness and death into their bodies, something that God never intended for them; it also brought a severing of their relationship with God, and this has been passed down through the generations ever since.

God has always intended for us to walk with Him, to know Him and be in relationship with Him, just as Adam and Eve were at the beginning. However, God is perfect and we aren't, and it's our imperfections, our bad behaviour and self-centeredness that keep us separate from Him.

In spite of this, God's love for us is so great that He has made a way for us to draw near to Him.

He came to Earth as a person, named Jesus, and because He was God He was perfect in every way. The plan was that even though Jesus was without fault he would die through crucifixion, the worst punishment of all. He willingly did this, taking the penalty for everyone's sins and wrongdoing, knowing that it would release us from the devil's trap and give us the opportunity to live closely with God again. All we have to do is acknowledge that we have turned our back on God, done things wrong and in our own way in our lives, and accept that Jesus has taken the punishment for us. God will forgive us and accept us; just start talking to Him and be honest and sincere.

Like Adam and Eve in the Garden of Eden, we too have the voice of the serpent, the devil, talking into our spirits, trying to convince us that God isn't real or that the Bible, His word, isn't true. Which voice are you listening to?

To show that God has accepted us and that we will always live with Him, once we turn back to Him he places inside us His Holy Spirit. This confirms with our own spirit that we belong to Him – that reassurance we have that we are a child of God and He is our heavenly Father.

If you have never acknowledged that Jesus died for you I invite you to take a few moments now. Ask God to forgive all that you have done wrong in your life and accept that Jesus took the punishment in your place. Remember to thank Him. Now tell someone what you've done. The Bible says:

1 John 1:9
If we claim to be without sin we deceive ourselves and the truth is not in us. If we confess our sins He is faithful and just and will forgive our sins and purify us from all unrighteousness.

If you have taken this step, your life is with God, here on earth and in heaven. You have been purified, you've got a clean sheet, and your future is secure. Congratulations!

For Further Reflection

John 3:16
For God so loved the world that He gave His one and only son, that whoever believes in Him shall not die but shall have eternal life.

1 John 5:12
He who has the son has life, he who does not have the son of God does not have life.

2 Corinthians 5:17
If anyone is in Christ he is a new creation; the old has gone, the new has come.

Chapter Two

Damaged Goods

I wish I could say that I was born into a loving, secure, Christian family where all my needs were met, but that just wasn't the case. I was the fourth child in a family of five, and my earliest memory was being in a pram in the rain, feeling cold and my mother shouting at me. I don't ever remember my mother holding me or even putting her arm around me, and I don't believe I had a healthy or affectionate bonding to her. When I was eighteen months old my younger brother was born, and his personality was quite different from mine in that he wasn't afraid to demand attention. Rejection was one of my early experiences, and being a naturally compliant child I soon learned to keep quiet and just get on independently – two coping strategies that served me effectively for many years.

In addition to my ability to be extremely quiet and independent, there were two other characteristics I possessed: competitiveness and determination. The combination of independence and determination has been a key factor in overcoming obstacles in my walk through life.

My relationship with my dad was a saving grace; the only problem was that I didn't see him very often as he worked long hours as a pharmacist. I have many good memories of him and, unlike my mother, I do remember sitting on him and having cuddles. He read stories to my younger brother and me, was full of interesting information, and I remember one day being fascinated as I watched him dissect a worm on the kitchen table. He would take us out for walks along the country lanes, especially during the blackberry season, or to the park; and I loved watching and listening to him playing the piano at home.

We didn't have any extended family apart from my dad's parents, who were elderly and lived nearly two hundred miles away in Liverpool. In addition to my parents, the other key person at home who left a lasting impact on my life was a brother seven years older than I, who was a constant bully throughout my childhood and into my teen years until he finally left home. From as early as I can remember I was frightened when I saw him or heard his voice.

I think being the victim of bullying left its mark, and as I grew up I realised I had a zero tolerance level when it came to bullying. In fact the only time in my life I remember responding violently to a situation was at school as a fifteen-year-old when I saw a senior schoolboy bullying a first year girl during a lunch break. Without too much thought I went up and punched him hard in the mouth, splitting his lip so it bled. My friends who were watching were worried that he would get his friends to retaliate, but I think he was too stunned to admit to anyone that a girl half his size could hurt him.

Looking back at my home life and the constant bullying from my older brother, one thing that has been hard to comprehend is that everyone at home knew he treated me badly and it was just accepted and not challenged.

Unfortunately, by the time I was eight my parents divorced, and little did I realise that it would be thirty-one years later before my dad and I were reunited. However much I used to believe that the divorce hadn't affected me, it is true to say that the circumstances around that time and the loss I experienced have had a big impact on my life and my relationships.

It's commonly accepted in the area of psychology and counselling that children around the age of eight who experience the loss of a parent will often feel guilty, as if it was their fault. In addition to the hidden feelings of guilt, I was convinced that I wasn't important or even wanted and valued by my parents. After I became a Christian I couldn't understand why God had let me be born into such an unhappy family environment if He loved me, and I projected my feelings of not being loved onto Him, wrongly believing that love meant I should have had a smooth life; I deduced that God didn't really love me either.

There are so many passages in the Bible that speak of God's love for us, even the fact that He sent Jesus to die in our place so we could live in a close relationship with Him, but although I could accept this love on an intellectual level, I was unable to feel it deep inside. It's hard to feel something spiritual that hasn't been experienced in physical human terms. I started to focus on what I didn't believe rather than on what I knew was true, and this resulted in me wanting to walk away from God. What was interesting was that the more I was unhappy with God, the more I talked to Him telling Him how unhappy I was. Without realising it, as I continued to talk to Him I was in constant prayer with Him, for prayer is simply communicating with God.

I behaved immaturely, rather like a toddler trying to get its own way and pushing at the boundaries. I decided to go on an open-ended fast until I heard from God, as if that would twist His arm and make Him give me the answers! All I wanted was to know why if God loved us there was suffering in the world, and particularly why *I* had suffered. The more silent God was, the more I kept accusing Him of not being fair or true to His word.

What I overlooked was that God knows us more than we can imagine; after all, He created us.

He won't be manipulated, but He does care and won't let go of us. I started to remember the words of a hymn that I used to sing at school: "Oh, love that wilt not let me go... Oh, joy that seekest me through pain." God was gently drawing me back to Himself. It was I who had turned my back, and increasingly I knew deep within that I wouldn't receive the answer to my question at that time. What I needed to do was just to trust God and turn around so He could embrace me. I had to put away my pride and accept God on His terms and not mine.

The outcome of this experience is that I've never since doubted that God is with me and that He cares for me, even when I don't understand and haven't got all the answers, and even when I'm not my best. Just as little children don't understand everything but have to be obedient to their parents who *do* know what's best for them, so we have to follow what God says with a childlike belief that He knows what's best for us. If there's something I don't understand, I've learned that in time I will, for as I mature spiritually He will give me the understanding and knowledge in His timing, not mine. It's not about what we do; it's about what God does, and we are safe with Him. What a relief!

Whatever you feel, nothing can change the fact that God *does* love you and always will. Look at your life. Don't focus on what you didn't have or haven't got; look at all that God *has* provided and be grateful. I know that throughout my life God has always given me good friends that have filled in some of the love gaps that I've had from my parents' inability to show love. Has God not also provided some good friends and family members for you along the way?

Pain from past hurts can result in us taking a step back from trusting people again, including trusting God. It's easy when we've been hurt to cover up the pain, not acknowledge it, partly because it's painful and partly because we don't have the ability to heal our inner wounds by ourselves. Burying the pain rather than facing it results in anger. The sequence is always: Event » Pain » Anger. We often think it's: Event » Anger. We think, "That made me angry," or, "They made me angry," but that's not the case. It's not a situation or person that causes anger; it's what we say to ourselves about the action or event that can result in anger. Cognitive behaviour therapy confirms this and teaches that if we adjust our thinking about a situation or circumstance then our feelings can also alter; we don't have to become angry. Often we are so good at skipping over our hurt in a fraction of a second, because it is painful and unpleasant, that we don't feel it; we just feel the anger.

Behind every feeling of anger is an unresolved hurt that needs to be acknowledged. What tends to happen if we don't deal with the hurt is that the next time something painful happens we can overreact;

the original unresolved hurt is still active within us and the two hurts add together to form a greater reaction. We can all think of people who fly into a fit of rage at the slightest thing; road rage is a good example of this. I overreacted when I punched the schoolboy. He didn't deserve all my anger; it was coming from the pain and anger I harboured relating to my bullying brother, though I was not consciously aware of this at the time. This is called projection – when we put something onto someone that doesn't belong. My aggression towards the schoolboy wasn't right or acceptable. I could make lots of excuses, but really there was no excuse; I just lost control of myself.

If there are times in your life that you remember feeling rejected and hurt, forgive the people that have hurt you and give God your pain. If there are memories or issues that cause anger to rise within when you think about them, then don't be afraid to recognise them, asking God to forgive all the times you've inappropriately expressed your anger and to help you acknowledge the pain so He can heal it for you. Be careful not to project your anger where it doesn't belong. Make a decision not to harbour anger again in your heart but to be bold and face the inner pain, knowing that there is nothing that God can't heal – and He wants to.

Have you ever had times when you get angry quickly even though you don't want to? Afterwards you are full of regret, ashamed, and vow never to react again, but it *does* happen again. I was like that once and I found a way to stop: I decided that anytime I felt angry I would open my Bible and start reading; and if I was out and didn't have a Bible to hand I would either have a Bible verse on a card in my pocket or I'd think of one quickly. It didn't matter what the verse was, I just turned straight to God's word. My logic was that if it was the devil that was tempting me, then he would soon back off if his action was sending me more and more to God's word. It worked.

Unchecked anger is very dangerous. It can lead to murder, and there are many occasions when a person has murdered without meaning to (usually considered manslaughter) – they simply lost control of themself. None of us are immune to this extreme if we fail to address our angry reactions. Yet this is not the only danger with unchecked anger; there is another issue which is far more common and that is depression. I'm aware that I run the risk of offending when I say this and that's not my intention. I'm no expert on depression, but the more I experience depressed people the more I'm convinced that behind the discouraging feelings of depression there lurks unexpressed hurt and anger. There are many good books written on depression and overcoming this, and space limits what I can include here, but suffice to say that anyone feeling depressed is suffering, like being in a deep dark pit that seems to have no exit; God wants to heal the pain and release the person from their suffering. I too have suffered times of depression – thankfully only for short periods and I was always determined to find a way forwards. One of my methods of overcoming was to make a decision to go and help someone else; it's hard to feel bad when you're focused on someone else's problem. The devil will try to convince you that there is no hope; don't believe it!

Mark 10:27
All things are possible with God.

If you know you have feelings of hurt and anger about a situation, I recommend that you tell a wise and trusted friend so they can pray with you. The act of telling someone is a step towards trusting, and the more one does this the easier it becomes. It may seem strange at first, maybe even the opposite of what you want to do, but believe me, it will have a lasting impact on how you feel and relate to others. Independence and pride can be obstacles that get in the way of trusting people; don't let that prevent you from receiving the full freedom and release that God intends for you.

For Further Reflection

John 10:28
I give them eternal life and they shall never perish, no-one can snatch them out of my hand.

Proverbs 3:5
Trust in the Lord with all your heart and lean not on your own understanding.

Romans 8:38-39
Neither death nor life, neither angels nor demons, neither the present nor the future nor any powers, neither height nor depth, nor anything else in all creation, will be able to separate us from the love of God.

Chapter Three

Learning to Receive Love

One thing I hadn't realised as a young adult was how much our early experiences in life programme us to respond in certain ways to situations. Thankfully, when we recognise this we can chose to change our responses – there's no such thing as being stuck with what we are – and God will help us to improve.

During my childhood I was constantly being blamed for what seemed like everything! As an active child it wasn't uncommon for me to get cuts and bruises, and I was never comforted when I hurt myself – only criticised for being careless. I developed a sensitive conscience that self-blamed to the point that I didn't tell anyone if I hurt myself because I knew it had to be my own fault. Even from an early age, if I fell over and cut myself I would get the first aid kit from the kitchen and hide away in a quiet corner, clean the wound and put a plaster on. I knew how to look after myself.

One sunny day when I was six years old, as I skipped back to school, having been home for lunch, I tripped up on the pavement and cut my knees. Almost immediately after getting to my feet a bee stung my arm. The journey back to school took just five minutes yet I entered the playground looking like I'd been in a battle and feeling quite sore. To make things worse, because I couldn't hide the blood that was running down my legs, I knew I had to tell my teacher. I wasn't crying – I'd already learned to accept pain – but I was scared that I would be in trouble for hurting myself, that it was all my fault. What I actually discovered and found quite remarkable was that the teachers were nice to me. They cleaned the wounds, talked gently to me, and I didn't feel bad at all. How strange, I thought!

A few years later I had another experience resulting in far greater pain and sense of isolation. I always enjoyed running, jumping, skipping and generally being active; walking properly in an orderly fashion was really not normal for me. Roller skating became a favourite activity of mine, and one of my sisters, who was three years older than I, also skated. When I was nine years old I was able to skate faster than her, and at that point she gave me a challenge I couldn't resist and will always remember.

We lived on a corner at the bottom of a hill, and I was very content to skate down the last part of the hill, just a short distance and around the corner. My sister, however, was able to skate all the way from the top of the hill. I'd never considered doing this – maybe I instinctively knew my limits – until one day my sister said, "I'll call you a baby if you don't try it." Well, how could I ignore a challenge like that? So I devised a strategy: I would stop at each lamppost coming down the hill on the first few attempts to get used to it, especially if I thought I was going too fast, and then I'd do it all the way without stopping. One quiet afternoon when no-one was looking I nervously made my way to the top of the hill and started the descent. Approaching the first lamppost and travelling extremely fast I decided to put my plan into action and stop at the lamppost. What I didn't understand was the power of momentum, and although I put my arms out to stop myself, they were not strong enough and I crashed into the lamppost at full speed! I'm not quite sure how I descended the rest of the hill – I think I took my skates off and walked – but I clearly remember the first evening, just a few hours after the accident, lying on the settee in agony, waiting for the doctor to arrive and give the news that I'd severe internal abdominal bruising that would take a few weeks to resolve.

I wasn't taken to hospital – my mother wouldn't let us be taken there – but our doctor visited three times during the first twenty-four hours to check on my condition. As I lay on the settee in pain my mother and oldest sister were standing in the room some distance away, talking, and I kept

One sunny day when I was six years old, as I skipped back to school, having been home for lunch, I tripped up on the pavement and cut my knees. Almost immediately after getting to my feet a bee stung my arm. The journey back to school took just five minutes yet I entered the playground looking like I'd been in a battle and feeling quite sore. To make things worse, because I couldn't hide the blood that was running down my legs, I knew I had to tell my teacher. I wasn't crying – I'd already learned to accept pain – but I was scared that I would be in trouble for hurting myself, that it was all my fault. What I actually discovered and found quite remarkable was that the teachers were nice to me. They cleaned the wounds, talked gently to me, and I didn't feel bad at all. How strange, I thought!

A few years later I had another experience resulting in far greater pain and sense of isolation. I always enjoyed running, jumping, skipping and generally being active; walking properly in an orderly fashion was really not normal for me. Roller skating became a favourite activity of mine, and one of my sisters, who was three years older than I, also skated. When I was nine years old I was able to skate faster than her, and at that point she gave me a challenge I couldn't resist and will always remember.

We lived on a corner at the bottom of a hill, and I was very content to skate down the last part of the hill, just a short distance and around the corner. My sister, however, was able to skate all the way from the top of the hill. I'd never considered doing this – maybe I instinctively knew my limits – until one day my sister said, "I'll call you a baby if you don't try it." Well, how could I ignore a challenge like that? So I devised a strategy: I would stop at each lamppost coming down the hill on the first few attempts to get used to it, especially if I thought I was going too fast, and then I'd do it all the way without stopping. One quiet afternoon when no-one was looking I nervously made my way to the top of the hill and started the descent. Approaching the first lamppost and travelling extremely fast I decided to put my plan into action and stop at the lamppost. What I didn't understand was the power of momentum, and although I put my arms out to stop myself, they were not strong enough and I crashed into the lamppost at full speed! I'm not quite sure how I descended the rest of the hill – I think I took my skates off and walked – but I clearly remember the first evening, just a few hours after the accident, lying on the settee in agony, waiting for the doctor to arrive and give the news that I'd severe internal abdominal bruising that would take a few weeks to resolve.

    I wasn't taken to hospital – my mother wouldn't let us be taken there – but our doctor visited three times during the first twenty-four hours to check on my condition. As I lay on the settee in pain my mother and oldest sister were standing in the room some distance away, talking, and I kept thinking, "If only my dad were here, he would know how to stop the pain." No-one spoke reassuring words to me or held me, and I didn't cry; I knew it must have been my fault and I just had to get on with it.

This painful experience and associated feelings were hidden away in my memory; it was my automatic response to pain and a way of coping.

Many years after that accident I had an amazing experience of healing. I started to remember the evening when I was lying in pain on the settee and so needing to feel loved and secure, and I started to cry. These were the tears that I hadn't been able to shed at the time, and through the tears I saw in my mind Jesus standing very close to me where I lay. As I had this revelation of Jesus being there with me, the tears stopped and the emotional hurt associated with these memories just disappeared. The wonderful thing about God is that He is omnipresent – the God of the past, present and future – therefore He can reveal Himself to us at any point in our lives and bring healing, even of past hurts and memories.

Our enemy, the devil, will do all he can to cause destruction in our lives. He targets us when we're young, so we establish patterns of behaviour and negative responses at an early age that, if not addressed, can stay with us throughout our life. Injury and pain, both physical and emotional, are key strategies to trap us in a cycle of self-protection and avoidance of any situations that could potentially cause further pain. When God created us He didn't intend us to suffer pain and definitely not to be alone. It is only by allowing ourselves to be vulnerable and accept help from others that we can truly live a full life and receive love. When we decide to be independent, to protect ourselves from injury or stay apart from relationship with others, we not only limit pain and hurt, we also limit the good feelings of experiences and relationships and of being loved, which includes the amount of love we are able to experience from God.

Are you the sort of person that would rather cope alone than call a friend when you're hurting? Do you say things like, "I'm alright," when clearly you're not? I used to be there myself, and I discovered that it stopped me feeling God's love. The extent that you block out the bad feelings, to that extent you also block out good feelings. I came to the realisation that if I wanted to experience more love from others and particularly God, then I had to choose to allow myself to be vulnerable rather than protective, and trust that even if I did get hurt, God could and would take the pain away.

My early experiences of dealing with pain on my own had led me to believe that I was self-sufficient, not needing anyone else. It is true that we all have within us an extraordinary ability to cope in times of stress, but that doesn't mean we have to live our lives in isolation. Far from it; when God created

Adam He said, "It is not good for man to be alone, I will make a helper for him." (Genesis 2:18)

Jesus did not live alone; he was in constant communication with God as his Father, and he also had plenty of friends and three close disciples that he shared his deepest thoughts and feelings with. In contrast to this, some people teach that everyone already has all that they need within them; I take issue with this type of teaching for I believe that although we do have within us the personality and gifts we need, they are activated in the presence of relationships not in isolation. It is through our relating that we develop and grow.

In my experience, sometimes the people that tend to stay isolated, believing they can look after themselves, are also the ones who are quick to criticise others and complain that there's no-one there when they need help. They become their own worst enemy. On the other hand, people who have healthy trusting relationships are more likely to have and accept help when they need it and are not so lonely. It's much easier to be with someone who can receive than with someone who is self-protective and closed to receiving.

So how is it possible to move from a position of self-sufficiency and isolation to one of receiving and feeling loved at a deeper level? I believe one of the first steps is to learn to value yourself as a person, to start believing that you are worth someone else's time and love, and for this you need to know how valuable you are in God's eyes. Knowing God loves you personally – after all, He chose to create you, didn't He? – and believing that He will provide all you need is the starting point. When God created me, He knew ahead of time all that I would experience and the struggles I'd have. He could have said, "This one's going to be hard work; I don't think I'll bother." But He didn't. He knew that He'd put inside me all I needed to overcome the obstacles, and He provided the right people at the right times in my life to help fill in the gaps. I'm not more special than you; it's the same for you too. What I found helped was spending time each day reading what the Bible says; find out for yourself how God sees you by what He says in the Bible. Using a concordance can help you discover some amazing verses, and I used to write my favourites on a card and keep it with me to help me remember. If you don't have a concordance, see if you can borrow one from church – this is also a step towards being open to receive help from someone, and the more times you practice, the easier it gets.

Write a list of all the times in your life when someone was there for you, whether you accepted their help or not. I did this and was blown away by the number of people God had placed in my life at just the right time. One day, as I was considering this, I suddenly remembered a lovely lady who was the playground supervisor at my primary school. She always had an apple for me in her coat pocket. I was

LEARNING TO RECEIVE LOVE

eight, going on nine, it was during the time my parents divorced, and I would often stand with her at playtimes, not wanting to talk but just holding her hand and eating the apple. She would tell me that she couldn't bring everyone an apple, and I felt very special. As I remembered this I realised that holding her hand was the only physical affection I had at that time in my life. God knew how to provide what I needed.

Sometimes we think we're alone when we're not at all; we just have blinkered vision and see the emptiness rather than the gift.

John 1:9
The light shines in the darkness and the darkness cannot overcome it.

There is no such thing as total darkness; there is always the light of God's love somewhere, but there are times we cannot see it. Nowadays, if I'm having a tough time I'll say to myself, "I know there's the light here somewhere; I just need to find it," and I'll ask God to show me the light. He always does! How much better it feels looking for a light that must be there rather than feeling overwhelmed by darkness and our circumstances.

Ask God to show you if there's anything that's getting in the way of you experiencing love and particularly *His* love. If anything comes to mind then tell a friend and ask them to pray with you. You may feel vulnerable, but this is a good step towards trusting again. Sometimes it takes a few hours or days to recognise God revealing hidden hurts to you. Don't be concerned and don't start looking for things. If He needs to remind you of something He wants to heal He will do that in His own perfect way and His own perfect timing, and with it He'll provide all that is required for your healing; He'll never let you down.

For Further Reflection

Isaiah 49:15-16
I will not forget you. See, I have engraved you on the palms of my hands.

2 Corinthians 1:3-4
Praise be to the God and Father of our Lord Jesus Christ, the Father of compassion and the God of all comfort, who comforts us in our troubles, so that we can comfort those in any trouble with the comfort we ourselves have received from God.

Psalm 94:18-19
When I said "my foot is slipping" your love, O Lord, supported me. When anxiety was great within me, your consolation brought joy to my soul.

Chapter Four

Healing of Bad Memories

Another time I experienced healing of memories was in relation to the six weeks I spent in foster care. A few weeks after my eighth birthday, my mother had to go into hospital for surgery. My younger brother, who was then six, and I were sent to a foster family just a short distance from where we lived, as my Dad was working long hours and couldn't look after us. My older brother and sister, being teenagers, were able to stay at home, and my other sister stayed with one of her friends. We didn't have any relatives that I was aware of except Granny and Granddad who were elderly and lived too far away.

The 'foster' family (I discovered many years later that they weren't registered foster carers) consisted of a boy, who attended the same junior school as I did and was a couple of years ahead of me, and his parents. On the first evening we all sat at the kitchen table for tea. I clearly remember being shown a cane that was in the corner of the room and being told that it would be used if we were naughty. That was a strange welcome to the home, particularly as we were well behaved children, and it set the tone for the rest of our time there.

During our six week stay we weren't taken to visit our mother in hospital even though the hospital had made it clear that children could visit. The family treated us unkindly, rather like slaves having to do unpleasant jobs for them, including clearing the driveway of snow each morning before we were allowed inside to have our breakfast, while they all stayed in the warm eating their breakfast. We also had to clean their son's rabbit hutch each week which always scared me as I had a fear of small animals, except for cats, as we had two at home.

I often heard threats from the foster parents that my dad wouldn't visit me if I wasn't good. This fear that I had to earn my dad's love was a barrier in later years in relationships, as I strived to be good enough to be loved, and particularly to earn God's love. My dad always visited on a Saturday evening after work, and I used to snuggle up to him on the settee to watch 'Dixon of Dock Green' which was my favourite programme. I pretended everything was alright and didn't ever tell him how awful it was staying there.

My memories of this experience were forgotten for many years until I was in my early thirties, when I gradually started to think about it again. I realised I could vividly remember the entire house, except for

HEALING OF BAD MEMORIES

the bedroom we slept in. I could remember the bedroom was located next to the bathroom, but for some reason I couldn't recall the layout inside the room even though I could remember the other rooms. I didn't understand why until God started to gradually allow the memories that had been so painful at the time to surface; I'd buried them deep down, suppressed them, in my subconscious mind.

This is what I started to remember:

I hadn't missed my mother while she was in hospital; it was only my dad that I wanted. My brother was different. He was used to our mother's attention and was finding it difficult to be without her. In the daytime he soiled his pants and at bedtime he would get upset and start crying.

Afraid of the foster parents and not wanting my brother to get into trouble, I devised a plan. I made him go into the bathroom first in the evening to have a wash and change into his pyjamas and on return to the bedroom give me his pants. I would then go and have my wash, and while in the bathroom I'd wash his pants and wring them out in my towel to remove much of the water so they wouldn't drip. I'd then hide them behind the radiator in the bedroom so they could dry without anyone seeing them.

There were twin beds in the room, and each night when I turned the light off, before my brother had time to get upset and start crying, I'd climb into his bed and cuddle him. We'd slide under the bedclothes so we weren't heard, and I'd whisper him stories – funny stories that made him laugh, as I discovered that if he was laughing he didn't cry. My dad always read stories to us at night, and I used to think that he'd be proud of me making up my own stories. I stayed in bed with my brother until he fell asleep, then I'd get back into my own bed.

One day I think the pressure of coping alone and my unhappiness all became too much, and I remember walking down the stairs with a deep sense of loneliness and abandonment. I couldn't tell anyone – there was no-one to tell – and I couldn't cry. My ability to keep quiet, blame myself and bury my feelings was all I had to keep strong and determined to survive during that time.

As God led me back in my thoughts to recall this experience, I started to remember that time of walking down the stairs devastated by loneliness and sense of being abandoned, a bit like watching a video of myself, and in my recollection I always stopped before I pictured myself reaching the bottom of the stairs. The pain of loneliness was overwhelming and I cried each time I remembered this experience. These were the tears that I'd buried long ago and were now surfacing. Then one day I sensed God say to me that the next time I thought about it I was to let the 'video' finish and keep walking to the bottom of the stairs in my mind's eye. So the next time the memory came to my thoughts again, even though it felt painful and I cried, I overcame my painful emotions and kept going, right to the bottom of the stairs. It was only then that I had an amazing vision: I could see Jesus standing at the bottom of the stairs with His arms open wide for me. In my mind's eye I ran into His arms, and in that instance the pain was gone. He had been there with me all the time with the love and security I needed – I just didn't know.

This healing experience developed in me a greater ability to trust, not only God but others too. You see, I'd discovered that no matter how much a person or an event could hurt me, or however long ago the experience was, God could always heal the memory and remove the pain. I didn't need to protect myself any longer from being hurt by other people. How releasing and empowering that knowledge was!

I started to consider that if God could completely take away inner emotional pain from many years back, how much more He will comfort me in any present situation that is painful. All I have to do each time I'm feeling hurt is to take my pain and upset to God immediately. This will prevent suppression of feelings, which is destructive, and without a shadow of doubt I know that God will remove the pain and replace it with an overwhelming sense of His love. This was a vital step that helped me to start receiving love in a deeper way from others without protecting myself for fear of pain and rejection. I learned that I didn't need to concern myself with whether I could trust others; I know people will hurt and offend at times even though it is mostly not intended, but I have a loving heavenly Father who can make anything and everything better.

Painful memories can be a stumbling block to us living a full life, trying new things or trusting people, as we can develop a self-protective barrier that will keep us away from similar situations that have the potential to cause us further pain and hurt. Rejection is something we all experience, and if this isn't balanced with unconditional acceptance then we can establish a fear of rejection and this too can result in avoidance of people and situations.

Erik Erikson, a psychologist famous for his theory of psychosocial development, suggests that we develop trust and security during our first year of life, gained from consistent dependability from our parents or carers. Without this we are likely to develop mistrust and fear of people and our environment.

Right from the moment of birth we have a need to be loved and held in addition to our physical needs of warmth and food. For some people, including myself, these emotional needs were not adequately met and I developed a deep sense of mistrust of people and a crippling feeling lasting into my adult years of needing to be held.

However long ago bad experiences happened, the memories can be healed, and one of the ways

God heals is to show us where He was at the time we experienced the painful event, supernaturally revealing this to us. For some people this could be as far back as the day they were born. I remember the amazing healing power of God's revelation when I realised that at my birth it didn't matter whether my parents wanted me, as God was there to receive me into His loving arms the moment I entered this world.

Isaiah 43:1-2

...he who created you ... he who formed you [says], "Do not fear, for I have redeemed you; I have summoned you by name; you are mine. When you pass through the waters, I will be with you."

I realised that this verse was speaking about God knowing me in the womb and then being present when I passed through the birth waters. This revelation established in me a deep sense of my value in God's eyes resulting in the feeling of being wanted and important, a miraculous change from how I had previously felt.

Before we can experience God's healing from past hurts we need to recognise and admit that there is a memory that still causes us pain when we think or talk about it. The pain may not be felt or expressed in terms of hurt; sometimes it can be disguised in feelings of anger, cynicism, blame of others, depression or even excessive humour. Before God can heal we have to acknowledge we have a need and ask Him to help us.

I remember once sitting at home on my bed conscious that if I were to progress in my relationship with God then I needed to trust Him more. I had become aware that I was being held back by fear of rejection, and I knew I had to overcome this.

I drew a picture to express my dilemma. As I did, the voice of my inner self became more apparent and I wrote underneath the picture: "I am afraid to be dependent on or need somebody because the hurt is too painful when I lose them. I have to stay within the limits of what I can handle as I've always had to cope with it alone. Taking risks of close relationships goes outside of what I can handle."

Jeremiah 31:3-4
I have loved you with an everlasting love; I have drawn you with loving kindness. I will build you up again and you will be rebuilt.

God can and will, if you are willing, guide you along the path of healing of past memories. This can be done alone or with someone else with you, and I would recommend having a trusted person to support and pray with you if you're not experienced with inner healing. Often, sharing your story or just

HEALING OF BAD MEMORIES

being quiet, waiting and listening to God is all that's required. It is then that the pain may start to rise from within, sometimes with crying. Don't hold it back, but let it flow and keep focused on the fact that God loves you so much and that any pain is only temporary, a cleansing of the inner wound so it can heal. You're not alone – God is with you all the way.

As the pain is released it is replaced with calmness, maybe a sense of relief that is God-given, and with it comes the knowledge that healing has taken place. God speaks to us in different ways because we are all different. I'm a very visual person so God often speaks to me through pictures and what I see.

Make sure you seal the healing by thanking God, telling someone else and testifying to what God has done for you. Also walk in the healing – by that I mean, don't let anything stop you from taking the risk of trusting again. Trusting is a decision you need to make if you want to progress with your relationships, and if this is an area you want to develop then start with small steps, trusting in small things and increasing as your belief and confidence that God can remove any hurt grows. If, however, you still can't trust then you may need to seek support from an experienced Christian.

A word of caution: if you've experienced or witnessed a very traumatic event, it is possible you need someone trained and experienced in post-traumatic stress counselling to help you. Let God lead you, and don't make yourself recall the experience unless a trained person is with you. There are special ways for dealing with the memory of traumatic events, and it's possible to make yourself worse if you try to 'go it alone'. God will miraculously heal, but He does expect us to use our common sense – so stay responsible.

For Further Reflection

Hebrews 13:5
[God has said:] Never will I leave you, never will I forsake you.

Isaiah 40:11
He gathers the lambs in His arms and carries them close to His heart.

Lamentations 3:22-24
Because of the Lord's great love we are not consumed, for His compassions never fail. They are new every morning; great is your faithfulness. I say to myself, "The Lord is my portion therefore I will wait for Him"

Chapter Five

Forgive? Why Wouldn't I?

In my early years as a Christian I was obsessed with knowing more of God. I was frequently listening to and singing worship songs, talking to Jesus, reading my Bible, reading any book that explained the Bible, and meeting regularly with other Christians to talk about... yes, you guessed it – God! It's easy to be full of joy when things are going well, but there came a time when my faith began to be tested.

I was in hospital following what was supposed to be minor surgery; however, things don't always go as planned, and my anticipated two-day stay turned into more complex surgery and ten days in hospital. My husband had taken time off work to look after the children: my son, who was nearly a year old, and my three-year-old daughter. In those days nurses and medical staff had the luxury of a side room when admitted to hospital, and I was grateful for this – the quiet surroundings and the personal bathroom. In fact, for someone who likes being independent, I wouldn't have managed very well on the open ward. It was all I could do to walk the few feet across my room to the bathroom by myself, slowly and holding on to whatever I could, as I was in pain each time I stood up and walked. After every visit to the bathroom I would carefully climb back onto the bed and, sinking into the pillows, I would pour out my gratitude to God for helping me – and the pain would subside. This expression of gratitude when my head hit the pillow was something that I've never stopped, and since that time in hospital in 1982 I've always told God everything I'm grateful for each night as I lay my head on my pillow before going to sleep.

The day of discharge came. It was a Sunday, and I was lying on the hospital bed listening to the morning service on the radio. As the service finished I felt restless, wanting more of something though I didn't know what. I decided to go to the hospital chapel and, after obtaining permission from the nursing staff, I went straight to the lifts and down two floors to get there. I wasn't sure what to do when I arrived; it was empty and I stood for a moment. Then I noticed the Bible open at the front, and I boldly walked forward to read it. Without a thought I started reading aloud. It was open at John chapter 14, and the words came alive as I spoke them:

John 14:1-3,14,16,18,21b
Do not let your hearts be troubled. Trust in God, trust also in me. In my Father's house are many rooms; if it were not so I would have told you. I am going there to prepare a place for you. And if I go and prepare a place for you, I will come back and take you to be with me that you also may be where I am ... You may ask me for anything in my name and I will do it ... I will ask the Father and He will give you another Counsellor to be with you for ever – the Spirit of truth ... I will not leave you as orphans, I will come to you ... he who loves me will be loved by my Father and I too will love him and show myself to him.

After I'd read the chapter I walked to the other side of the altar, knelt down and started crying. They weren't sad tears but tears of joy for what God was promising me. As I cried I started to remember the people in my life that had treated me badly and quite spontaneously, one by one, I forgave them. It was a remarkable time; I wasn't feeling upset or angry, but totally empowered by what I later discovered was the infilling of the Holy Spirit. Such a joy rose in me that I could hardly contain it, and that afternoon when I left the hospital I was still bubbling over.

This was an incredible experience and the beginning of my ability to forgive others no matter how much I was hurt. Forgiving isn't about who's right or wrong; it's about letting go, giving the person and situation to God and having the confidence that His love is so great and powerful that He can remove any pain that an experience has caused. We don't need to retaliate and get even in order to feel better.

Without releasing the person by the act of forgiveness, anger and bitterness will in time take the place of the hurt and detrimentally affect all relationships in life. As I learned more about forgiveness I realised that the only person I was hurting by not forgiving others was myself, and I decided there was no-one in my life that I wanted to hand over that power to, no matter what I'd suffered.

Does that mean forgiveness is easy? Of course not! Our natural self cries out for justice when we're hurt by another, and forgiveness often feels like a statement that says it doesn't matter. However, it *does* matter, and forgiveness is more about letting God deal with the person rather than accepting an injustice. Our hurts don't go unnoticed, and God will heal them if we let Him. I find it easier to forgive when I remember that God will take away the pain completely, but He generally does that *after* I've forgiven, not before, and the more I experience

God's healing, the more confidence I have in letting go and forgiving.

Through my life I've been hurt time and time again by my mother, and on each occasion since becoming a Christian I made the decision to forgive her and trust God with my pain. It hasn't always been easy, and sometimes I could only start by telling God I wanted to forgive but didn't know how to. In those instances God gradually gave me the ability, but it was I that had to take the first step, to bypass my emotions and speak the words of forgiveness, even if I didn't feel like it. Indeed, there were many times when I truly never wanted to see my mother again – but God always reminded me of the words in Ephesians:

Ephesians 6:2-3
Honour your father and mother – which is the first commandment with a promise – that it may go well with you and that you may enjoy long life on the earth.

I decided that being obedient to God and living a full life was more important to me than holding on to a grievance. I willingly allowed myself to be vulnerable in my mother's presence, to take whatever hurt came my way – and it did regularly – but I didn't allow it to take away my self-worth. In those moments I remembered that my confidence as a person had to come from God and not from what my parents said or thought of me.

Gradually, over the years, I found a way of coping with my mother, in addition to regular phone calls I'd visit once a month for a few hours when my children were at school. We'd have coffee or lunch out while shopping for clothes for my children. Those visits felt contained and relatively safe. I remember the first time I took my mother into a cafe, she was overwhelmed by the choice of coffees, and I suggested she try a cappuccino. She took a liking to these and it became a regular event each time we met.

Although she was getting on in years and in her eighties, when my mother suddenly passed away it was still a shock as she was quite active. I lived nearer to her than my siblings, just a fifty-mile drive up the motorway, and I had a key to her home. On return from a long weekend away visiting friends I was alerted to the fact that she hadn't been answering her phone for a couple of days. She'd passed away over the weekend and because, like many elderly people, she had locked and bolted her front door on the inside, I needed help from the police to break in and find her.

I didn't go inside and see her – the police advised not to, and as it was during a hot summer I had an idea what to expect. I knew I'd see her in the chapel of rest – I knew I *had* to, though at first I wasn't sure why.

FORGIVE? WHY WOULDN'T I?

A few days later the opportunity came to attend the chapel of rest. We'd been informed prior to our visit that the coffin was closed and we wouldn't be able to actually see my mother, a consequence of the hot weather and delay in finding her. Maybe this made it easier for me, I don't know, but once I was actually in the room with her, beside the coffin, I knew I needed to say everything that I'd never been able to say to her directly, so I could bring a closure to our relationship and the associated pain. There wasn't much to say – I'd already forgiven her and to a large extent forgotten many things – but for the first time ever I was able to state how hurt I'd been by her lack of love and her continual criticism and to *tell* her I'd forgiven her.

Then a strange thing happened. As I was able to be honest and speak out those thoughts, a feeling from deep inside me started to stir. It was a feeling of love for her, of genuine unconditional love, and for the first time that I could recall I started to feel like I wanted my mum. This wasn't a bad feeling or a feeling of loss, but something rather natural. Three times I hugged the coffin, and the love for her kept flowing. I knew this was an amazing, divine, miraculous moment; nothing of me could have had the desire and power to do this without God's presence.

On leaving the chapel of rest I walked with my sister back to Mum's house. We still had a lot to do to clear the house and prepare for the funeral, but inside me was a warm feeling, the knowledge that God had given me the most unexpected gift: the gift of knowing how it feels to love my mum. During the clearing of her house I slept in her bed at night (it seemed pointless driving back down the motorway to my home each evening) and I appreciated the feeling of being near to her. I noticed that instead of resentment I was remembering good things about my mum; I was talking about her in a positive, caring way without a hint of the pain I used to feel. I believe this is a taste of what will come when we spend eternity together; heaven had arrived on earth!

I'm sure we can all think of someone we know who is bitter. They go over and over the same incidents and blame the world for how they're feeling. They appear to be waiting for everyone to change and meet their needs, and it's difficult and discouraging to spend any length of time with them.

I suggest that bitterness stems from an unforgiving heart, from holding on to the grievance or perceived grievance that once hurt or offended. Not one of us will walk through this life without being hurt by someone, and not one of us will live our lives without hurting someone. None of us are perfect and it's just the way it is.

I believe most of the pain that we experience from others isn't intentional; we can be offended by all sorts of things; for example, someone not noticing or speaking to us or a comment taken out of context or misunderstood. Likewise, the things we say or do can also be misunderstood. I sincerely believe my mother didn't realise how hurtful she was.

We need good relationships to thrive and develop; we were not meant to live in isolation. And if relationships are what we need to function effectively in this world, it's not surprising that the enemy, the devil, does all he can to break down these relationships. It's so easy to feel offended and we can't stop misunderstandings happening, but we can decide how we respond in these situations. Our power to overcome the enemy is in forgiving and letting go.

I like to think of the hurts we experience as thorns piercing our skin. It takes us by surprise and is painful, sometimes with bleeding, but it's not until the thorn is removed that full healing can take place. And when it is removed it won't hurt as much. Forgiveness is like removing the thorn – full healing of our heart can't take place until we've forgiven.

I appreciate that there are people who have experienced great injustice and painful events in their lives, and I recognise the courage it takes to pick oneself up and carry on. However, I still maintain that forgiveness is a non-negotiable decision we need to make if we want to be free and live life to the full.

Forgiveness releases God's love into the atmosphere. You only have to look at major disasters to see people of courage standing up and declaring they have forgiven the perpetrators and then watching how much they achieve in helping others.

One of the greatest challenges we face with our struggle to forgive is ourself; it's hard to forgive if our self-esteem or self-worth is low. There can be an inner voice whispering to us, saying we really did deserve it; and to make oneself feel better it's far easier to blame someone else, put them down and exalt ourselves above them. The remedy for this is to build our self-worth based on the truth of how God values us and not on our feelings, which can be misleading. Talk with God every day; tell Him about what has hurt you, then let go of it and focus on all the good things in your life and how He sees you, reading over and over the verses in scripture that speak of His unending love for you.

Psalm 147:3
He heals the broken hearted and binds up their wounds

For Further Reflection

Matthew 6:14-15
For if you forgive men when they sin against you, your heavenly Father will also forgive you. But if you do not forgive men their sins, your Father will not forgive your sins.

Galations 6:9
Let us not become weary in doing good, for at the proper time we will reap a harvest if we do not give up. Therefore as we have opportunity, let us do good to all people...

Psalm 30:5 (GNB)
Tears may flow in the night but joy comes in the morning.

Chapter Six

There's No Half Measure with God

Our thoughts can have a powerful effect on us, and it's often said that what we say about ourselves is what we become. As a child growing up we hear many statements said over us from authority figures in our life – some are positive and helpful, others negative and destructive, if we accept them.

We carry on saying these statements to ourselves without realising it, as we have a continual internal dialogue being played in our thoughts throughout each day. This is normal, but if we don't check what we're actually saying, then we could be making continuous negative statements over ourselves without realising it, and this will cause negative thinking and responses in addition to feelings of lowered self-esteem.

For some reason the negative comments and statements seem to have the ability to be remembered far more easily than the positive ones. At school I received positive comments from my teachers, but these were drowned out by the negative comments I received at home. Without realising it, by the time I was an adult I had a long list of negative statements I was continually saying to myself in my inner thoughts each day.

I started to call myself "half measure" because it seemed that whatever my situation I never experienced the full measure that it appeared everyone else had. By thinking this I was making two big mistakes. Firstly, I was making an assumption about others; how could I know what their circumstances were? Secondly, I was ignoring what the Bible says about how full and perfect God's love is for me. I was putting my own perspective above God's and, in effect, thinking I was more knowledgeable than Him. How arrogant of me!

An example of how this affected me was in my thinking about God's gift of the Holy Spirit. I knew that my earlier experience in the hospital chapel was one of being filled with the Holy Spirit, but I didn't understand why I hadn't also received the gift of tongues. This gift is a God-given ability to speak a heavenly language that is not learned and often not understood. It is a way of communicating with God spiritually when we don't know what to say or we're unable to express our thoughts in our own language. It seemed that everything I read about receiving the gift of the Holy Spirit also included the gift of tongues. I felt cheated, that God had only given me half measure. I didn't blame God; I blamed *myself* for not being good enough. The desire to receive the gift of tongues kept getting stronger within me and with it the belief that I wasn't good enough in God's eyes. I didn't realise it, but these feelings were a result of being rejected and not experiencing unconditional love as a child; I subconsciously thought I needed to earn God's love.

I kept reading the Bible, studying about tongues and the use of this gift, and earnestly praying for it – but nothing happened. I kept a journal; I did not write in it daily but only when I thought I had something important to note. This became an effective way for me to tap into my inner thoughts, to discover through pouring out my thoughts on paper what I was actually thinking deep down and to receive enlightenment regarding what God was saying to me, guided I believe by the Holy Spirit, who is always pointing us to Jesus through whom we can find healing.

One day I drew in my journal a picture expressing heaven. At one end of the page I drew everyone in heaven gathered around God – smiling, cheering, happy and loved. At the other end of the page I drew myself, sitting far away with my back to them. I wrote underneath, "God, when I get to heaven, you'll have to come and find me, because if I come to you and you don't want me, the pain will be far more than I could bear."

This picture highlighted my inner fear and expectation of rejection. The desire for more of God teachers, but these were drowned out by the negative comments I received at home. Without realising it, by the time I was an adult I had a long list of negative statements I was continually saying to myself in my inner thoughts each day.

I started to call myself "half measure" because it seemed that whatever my situation I never experienced the full measure that it appeared everyone else had. By thinking this I was making two big mistakes. Firstly, I was making an assumption about others; how could I know what their circumstances were? Secondly, I was ignoring what the Bible says about how full and perfect God's love is for me. I was putting my own perspective above God's and, in effect, thinking I was more knowledgeable than Him. How arrogant of me!

An example of how this affected me was in my thinking about God's gift of the Holy Spirit. I knew that my earlier experience in the hospital chapel was one of being filled with the Holy Spirit, but I didn't understand why I hadn't also received the gift of tongues. This gift is a God-given ability to speak a heavenly language that is not learned and often not understood. It is a way of communicating with God spiritually when we don't know what to say or we're unable to express our thoughts in our own language. It seemed that everything I read about receiving the gift of the Holy Spirit also included the gift of tongues. I felt cheated, that God had only given me half measure. I didn't blame God; I blamed *myself* for not being good enough. The desire to receive the gift of tongues kept getting stronger within me and with it the belief that I wasn't good enough in God's eyes. I didn't realise it, but these feelings were a result of being rejected and not experiencing unconditional love as a child; I subconsciously thought I needed to earn God's love.

I kept reading the Bible, studying about tongues and the use of this gift, and earnestly praying for it – but nothing happened. I kept a journal; I did not write in it daily but only when I thought I had something important to note. This became an effective way for me to tap into my inner thoughts, to discover through pouring out my thoughts on paper what I was actually thinking deep down and to receive enlightenment regarding what God was saying to me, guided I believe by the Holy Spirit, who is always pointing us to Jesus through whom we can find healing.

One day I drew in my journal a picture expressing heaven. At one end of the page I drew everyone in heaven gathered around God – smiling, cheering, happy and loved. At the other end of the page I drew myself, sitting far away with my back to them. I wrote underneath, "God, when I get to heaven, you'll have to come and find me, because if I come to you and you don't want me, the pain will be far more than I could bear."

This picture highlighted my inner fear and expectation of rejection. The desire for more of God didn't subside, and a few weeks later we attended the Spring Harvest annual Christian festival. Knowing I was facing an obstacle that I hadn't succeeded in overcoming, I decided to call on the help of the prayer ministry team and tell them about my 'half measure'. During the time with them, and with their gentle guidance and encouragement, as we prayed together I was able to start speaking in tongues and experienced an amazing, overwhelming, divine revelation that I was and always had been special to God. I was so happy; I knew for certain that the feeling of half measure had disappeared, and in its place was a belief that God really did love me as much as everyone else. This may sound crazy, but for the rest of that day (and indeed the rest of the week), at every opportunity between seminars, I kept going into the toilets to keep checking I could still speak in tongues and it hadn't disappeared!

It's natural to measure God's love for us by our experiences in human relationships. If our father had little time for us then we will naturally think that God has little time for us. If our parents had difficulty providing for us then it will naturally be harder for us to see God as our abundant provider. My thinking that God only wanted to give me half measure was fuelled by my false belief that I was not as worthy of His love as everyone else. How wrong I was!

Before I received the ability to speak in tongues, God didn't suddenly change His mind about whether He loved me; He had always loved me totally as much as everyone else. It was my belief about God that had to change; my perspective had to line up with the truth about God and my place in His family. If you ever feel like you're not as important to God as others, then know that it is a lie from the devil; it is possible for your beliefs to change and for you to feel God's love like never before.

Speaking in tongues is a gift to be practised and used daily. Primarily it is used for self-edification, and at first I hadn't appreciated how important to me it would become. With my newfound belief that God really did love me, I wanted to give something back to Him. At that time my children were school age so I made a decision that I would spend half an hour each day praying in tongues, even though I didn't know what I was saying. I scheduled protective time each morning from 9.15am to 9.45am, as soon as I'd dropped the children off at school, ensuring I didn't make arrangements to see anyone before 10am. This worked well, and for half an hour each day I knelt and prayed in tongues. Sometimes I felt nothing but was glad that I'd given the time to God. Other times I would start crying though I didn't know why. Through my tears I continued praying in tongues, and the crying always gave way to a sense of relief; I can only believe that God was healing and cleansing deep within me.

There's No Half Measure with God

Over the years I discovered that I needed the gift of tongues more than I ever imagined. I found that when I was afraid I had a tendency to freeze, unable to speak natural words. At those times it was remarkable that I was able to speak in tongues, sometimes only in a whisper, and the fear went. Often these fearful moments were times of actually feeling the presence of the devil close to me. Sometimes this would be during the night, suddenly waking from a scary dream or being aware of a cold shadow near me. Once the fear had gone I would fall asleep completely at peace. Nowadays it has become automatic for me to start speaking in tongues when I experience anything that disturbs me, whether during the day or night. I also use tongues when praying for healing as I need the Spirit's guidance to know how and what to pray.

Prior to receiving the gift of tongues, the self-declaration of half measure had been a negative statement declared over my life that had held me back. Words spoken are powerful – they have the ability to bless or curse – and as I learned more about the effect of our words, I started to replace my negative statements with positive ones. I also made sure I was reminded of positive statements during my day – for instance, as my online passwords to access personal internet sites, fridge magnets and cards which I kept in my pocket – so at every opportunity I was changing my thinking to bring it in line with what God said about me, rather than what I felt. It takes time and lots of practice, but the result of continuous positive affirmations is a positive mentality that will affect each area of life in a good way.

What do you say to yourself? Make a list of all the things you say. Highlight the positive statements and change the negative ones to a positive, then add more positive statements to your list from what God says about you in the Bible. Every day read these positive statements aloud until you start to believe them.

Another method I used was to play Christian songs and hymns that spoke of God's love. Still now I find that an old song I used to sing will just pop into my thoughts when I least expect it and give a boost of positive affirmation to my day. That's how God's Spirit works; He will remind us, but we have to first feed our minds with the truth.

Be aware though that positive thinking isn't about being unrealistic when your situation isn't good; it's about looking beyond the circumstances and not allowing yourself to be pulled down by anything that crosses your path. There is a time for singing and a time for crying, but whether we sing or cry our value as a person never diminishes nor changes.

For Further Reflection

1 Corinthians 14:1-2
Follow the way of love and eagerly desire spiritual gifts ... for anyone who speaks in a tongue does not speak to men but to God ... he utters mysteries with his spirit.

James 1:6
But when he asks he must believe and not doubt.

Matthew 7:11
If you then, though you are evil, know how to give good gifts to your children, how much more will your Father in heaven give good gifts to those who ask Him.

Chapter Seven

Don't Believe Everything You Hear

Apparently, during my pre-school years I was frequently ill. I had whooping cough as a baby and wasn't expected to live until the next day – which of course I did. Then I developed sensitivity to food and commenced a low fat, gluten free diet. I don't remember this diet, apart from having orange juice at school instead of milk, as I was able to tolerate most foods by the time I started school. However, I do remember growing up with the knowledge that my mother had to make separate food for me and how much more work that was for her, a subtle way my mother had of blaming me.

I was frequently told when growing up that as an infant I'd been described by doctors as "failure to thrive" because I was not increasing in weight as expected and kept falling asleep. In fact, the first couple of terms at school I only attended in the mornings; I would fall asleep when I went home for lunch, often before even eating lunch. The school didn't object to me missing half a day; there was always reading in the afternoon session, and as I read at home I was ahead in reading and didn't get behind with schoolwork. Looking back, with the knowledge I have now, I think falling asleep was my way of coping with stress rather than being a physical need. Even as an adult, when under a lot of pressure the first thing I think to myself is, "I'm tired," and I want to sleep.

In addition to these health issues, I developed frequent tonsillitis around the age of four years. It gradually resolved itself, but until then I had several choking fits during meals when I couldn't swallow properly; my mother would then shout at me, saying that I would still have to eat all my dinner even if I was sick in it!

I think it was a combination of these experiences that developed in me some inner scripts that I unconsciously said to myself for many years. One was "I hate food and it hates me!" Another was "I can't eat; I'm going to be sick." And yet another was "I'm tired." But the one that has had the most effect on me was "I'm no good."

It wasn't surprising then that as I reached teenage years, with a low self-esteem, I discovered a way to feel strong and in control: I stopped eating. I'd no knowledge of anorexia nervosa at that time; I just knew that if I secretly missed a meal I felt good. Added to this was the discovery that if I'd already eaten and then became upset by something, I could make myself sick, and this also made me feel good. What a dangerous road I was on without even knowing.

Thankfully, God is not surprised by anything we do and He always has in place for us all we need. For me it was the teachers at school. They were very positive and encouraging, and I guess they must have started to see concerning signs. One day after an orchestra practice, as I slowly collected my things (as slowly as I could so as not to get home too quickly), a teacher approached me. It was strange; he wasn't *my* teacher, he was from the Canary Islands on a year's placement to teach Spanish, but he started chatting and before long I'd begun to tell him how unhappy I was at home. Over the next few months he helped me talk about my problems and connected me to a Brazilian family visiting England for a year. He said I could help them learn English, but of course in doing this he'd provided a safe place for me to visit, relax and belong.

I was able to relate to this teacher quite easily and I admitted to him that I was missing meals, which resulted in him checking each day that I'd eaten school dinner. He was firm but not nasty; he became a father figure to me and helped me gradually get back to eating properly. I was internalising all he said and taught me, which means I could hear his voice and what he would say in a situation even if I wasn't with him. This ability I had to internalise helped me for many years and set me back on a better way. I believe it was God's guidance that enabled him to snatch me from the destructive path of anorexia nervosa that I'd inadvertently stepped onto.

Once into adulthood, and having convinced myself for many years that I was free from anorexia, I was surprised and ashamed to suddenly discover this was not the case. I was in a difficult marriage, and one evening after a stressful argument, without thinking, I sneaked away and made myself sick. I felt so ill for the rest of the night and guilty that I'd done this. It was like I couldn't stop myself, and I knew I needed to find someone to pray with me; only God's supernatural power could destroy this for good. However, there was a problem: each time I thought about telling someone, I felt a tightening in my throat, a feeling of being strangled and not being able to breathe, and this frightened me so much that I didn't know how to ask for help. But God is not put off by what we can't do; He knows our hearts. Without me being aware, God spoke to one of my friends through a word of knowledge that I needed help. My friend didn't know what the problem was, but this started a series of events that led to a full release and healing.

The healing and release came during a planned time of prayer. Some would call this deliverance and maybe it was; I believe deliverance and healing are closely related. It doesn't matter how it's categorised, what's important is what God does and the outcome. During the prayer time there came a moment when I started to cough. I was frightened, thinking I wouldn't be able to breathe, but I kept trusting that God was helping me, and the people with me were very loving and encouraging. Suddenly all the fear was gone and I felt different. It was very strange, like something of me was missing. Afterwards I went for a walk alone; I needed time to know who I was, I felt so different. I went to the swimming pool and stood on the balcony just watching the swimming for a long time, not recognising myself. I began to realise that the inner voice I'd known all my life that had continually said, "I'm no good," had gone. In its place was a deep sense of peace and the knowledge that God loved me so much that even when I couldn't get help for myself, He came to rescue me.

Later that week during a morning service of communion, surrounded by hundreds of other Christians, for some incredible reason that I can't explain, as I took the wine I managed to dramatically miss my mouth and spill the wine all over me. I had red wine all over my face, hands and clothes. In the past I would have felt so embarrassed by this but now it was different; I couldn't stop laughing as all I could think was, "I've been washed in the blood of the Lamb!" This was the beginning of a new me, one that laughed a lot, not as in the past to hide the pain but because I was free and loving life. No-one could take this freedom from me.

DON'T BELIEVE EVERYTHING YOU HEAR

Words are powerful; thoughts are powerful. They have the ability to build up or destroy. Many people just aren't aware of what they think or say; they make continuous negative statements over themselves, their family and friends without ever realising that there is a power in words that, if not checked, can become a self-fulfilling prophesy – and by that I mean we can become what we say we are. Whatever we've experienced in life, whatever has been said about us or over us, it cannot have any lasting power or effect if we choose to dismiss the negative and embrace positive thinking and statements.

The first step is to tune in to what your thoughts are saying – is it true, helpful and uplifting? If not, then change it. Remember that God created you and knows you far better than anyone else, so listen to what He says by reading the Bible. Read positive statements each day, morning and night; search for inspirational quotes on the internet or in books. Once you start looking you'll be amazed how much there is to find. At first it may seem like an exercise; after all, our negative thoughts have been with us for a while. Just persevere; the more you feed yourself good things the more you'll start thinking and feeling more positively. You'll not only notice what you're saying to yourself, but you'll notice how negative other people can be and will want to spend less time with them. Where possible, make sure the people you mix with most are positive and inspiring people.

I'm not ashamed that I've had times of being anorexic. I'm pleased that God designed us in such an amazing way that we have the ability to endure, protect ourselves and progress even through the hardest of times. For me, the way to feel any sense of control over increasingly difficult circumstances was to stop eating. Other methods commonly used can be withdrawing, attention seeking, having frequent illnesses, or dependency on alcohol or drugs. These coping mechanisms can work initially, but they all have a limited time when they are effective and then they start becoming destructive to us if not addressed.

There are lots of methods offered for overcoming these sorts of problems, but in my experience these are generally measures to control the situation rather than overcome. It is God who has the ability to completely heal, deliver and restore a person to the extent that they are completely free. That doesn't mean medical help and other rehabilitation programmes aren't helpful – of course they are, and many are to be recommended as part of the healing process – but ultimately it is God Himself who has the power to set people free.

For Further Reflection

Isaiah 38:16-17
You restored me to health and let me live ... in your love you kept me from the pit of destruction.

John 10:27-28
My sheep listen to my voice; I know them and they follow me, I give them eternal live and they shall never perish; no-one can snatch them out of my hand.

Psalm 31:7-8
I will be glad and rejoice in your love for you saw my affliction and knew the anguish of my soul. You have not handed me over to the enemy but have set my feet in a spacious place.

Chapter Eight

We Can Move Mountains

As my Christian life developed I became more and more aware that when I prayed with someone, God always seemed to do something good. I was also learning that with the Holy Spirit inside us we can access and utilise the power and authority of God, anytime and anywhere.

One Sunday morning, as I was walking in the rain the short distance to the hospice where I worked, I saw a dog coming towards me from the other end of the street. I'd always been nervous of dogs since a bad experience with an Alsatian when I was three years old, and this morning I started to feel fear rising within me. Rather than allow fear to take over, after a rapid prayer to God for His help (my shortest, most frequent prayer in a crisis moment that always works is, "Jesus help me!"), I suddenly thought of what I could do. When the dog was within a few feet of me, I pointed to the direction from where it had come and said in a bold authoritative voice, "Go back home!" The dog suddenly stopped walking and stood still, looking at me. Then I spoke again, more firmly this time and continued pointing in the direction from where it had come: "In the name of Jesus, I command you to go back home." The dog turned around and went back. Wow! I was not only relieved; I was amazed. This is the sort of thing you read about in the Bible; I didn't realise I could actually do it.

Just a few months after this amazing experience I was in Sierra Leonne, West Africa, working on a hospital ship. I was praying daily with patients, and we were seeing miraculous answers to prayer and healings.

One night, in the early hours, I woke with extreme abdominal pain. I'd developed dysentery and the pain was so bad I couldn't move. Suddenly I decided to do for myself what I'd often done for others: I put my hands over the pain and prayed, commanding the pain to go in the name of Jesus. I don't know why, but until that moment it had never occurred to me that I could pray in the same way for my own healing. After several minutes of prayer the pain gradually and miraculously subsided and I fell asleep. In the morning I began to realise what had happened, and my belief in our God-given ability to take command over situations increased rapidly, along with a greater awareness and love for God.

Back in England, and now into winter, I was driving home from work and it started snowing – big flakes that were falling and settling fast. I was on the country roads, staying away from the motorway rush hour, and was still about eleven miles from home. I could sense that if the snow kept falling like this I'd be stuck in a very short time and have to sleep in the car overnight; not a pleasant thought. I suddenly remembered reading in the Bible of how the disciples had been frightened in their boat during a storm and how Jesus had accused them of having little faith. I also remembered the time in Africa when I had prayed that night I was in pain and couldn't do anything else. I decided my faith was quite good, so I started to command the clouds to hold the snow. I said this boldly, raising one arm up as I spoke while still driving. After a few commands the snow stopped! I was now laughing and singing and I knew I would get home safely, though it did take me three hours. Even the clouds will obey!

With these experiences I increasingly came to believe that we do have the ability to pray for anything according to God's will and see results. I believe His will includes my safety, protection and healing. Following this my faith increased and with it my belief that with God's help I can do all things.

I think I needed these experiences to prepare me for the day when I was faced with a greater challenge. I was boarding a train in London to attend a work appointment and I started to feel acute abdominal pain. This wasn't the first time I'd experienced this pain as I'd had it a few times in the past. It was like gallstone pain; previously it had lasted between three to five hours and was always accompanied by excessive vomiting. This was not only excruciatingly painful, it was extremely inconvenient. I knew if I gave in to the pain I'd end up being taken by ambulance to a London hospital, not at all what I wanted, so I had no other alternative but to pray. Once I was aboard the train, and feeling like I would be sick at any moment, I went to the toilet. My train journey was just fifteen minutes and I had an urgency to get this sorted now. I put my hands on my abdomen and started praying, not asking God for anything, but just firmly commanding the pain and sickness to go. I pressed harder as I spoke authoritatively and as loudly as I dared, hoping that none of the other passengers could hear. After about six to seven minutes the sickness went and the pain started to subside. I felt safe to leave the toilet, and when I finally got off the train I walked the remainder of the journey to my appointment, praising God all the way. I'd been reminded again that day that there is nothing to stop us taking authority over our own sickness.

The Bible says that when we turn back to God and accept that Jesus died in our place for all our wrongdoing, God places inside us His Spirit, who confirms that we belong to Him and will teach, comfort and guide us through this life. The Spirit of God inside us is the same Spirit that powerfully raised Jesus from the dead. This means that we have an amazing Spirit within us who is so powerful that

He is capable of raising the dead! One great shame is that many Christians are still unaware of the power and potential of this Spirit within them. Can you imagine what could be achieved in the world if all Christians started to take authority over sickness in the same way as Jesus did when He was on the earth? Not only sickness, but we can also take authority over any aspect of our lives that obstructs and prevents us living in a divine, purposeful way.

It's so easy to see anything that goes wrong or frustrates us as a barrier or obstacle and then become discouraged and moan about it rather than see it as an opportunity to exercise our spiritual muscles and pray using the God given-authority we have. Each time we see challenges instead of problems we are creating an atmosphere of faith and belief. Gradually, the more we get used to this perspective, the more we will see astonishing things in our life. How exciting it would be if we were constantly tuned in to seeing God perform miracles each day. I believe that's what walking with God is all about: not about rituals of prayer meetings and fasting to gain points and ease our conscience (though, of course, I do believe prayer and fasting are vital parts of our life) but about walking and talking with God every minute of our day. It is about knowing that there is absolutely nothing that can separate us from the love of God (Romans 8:38-39).

For Further Reflection

Acts 3:16
It is Jesus' name and the faith that comes through Him that has given this complete healing.

Matthew 17:20,21
If you have faith as small as a mustard seed you can say to this mountain "move from here to there" and it will move. Nothing will be impossible for you.

1 Peter 2:24
By His wounds you have been healed.

Chapter Nine

False Accusations

I was fifteen and enjoying school and study. I loved sport and music, and every year I was in the school team for athletics, basketball, netball and rounders, and also in the school orchestra and choir. In the summer holidays I played in the county orchestra and band. In addition I loved Maths and Science and had decided that I wanted to be a surgeon. I was one of the rare breed of girls that enjoyed doing dissections in the lab! I was surrounded by many good friends and teachers, and school had become my 'home'; it felt safe and I was happy there.

Then one day it all changed. My mother decided to move away to a big city and in that moment I lost everything that was precious to me – including my identity, as she changed my name, replacing my dad's name for hers. I found myself in a very large comprehensive school over twice the size of my previous school, no teachers that I knew, no friends, no country walks – and it was disappointing that many of the subjects I had been studying for O-level didn't fit, either because the new school didn't teach them, as with Russian, or because I'd been studying a completely different syllabus, as with History. This meant that in some subjects I was ahead and in others I was behind. I was completely bereft, and I didn't know how to tell anyone.

There was, however, one big gain and that was in Music. As soon as my Music teacher heard me playing the flute she sent me to audition for a Saturday music school, and I passed with flying colours. The music school had excellent facilities and teaching, and enabled me to quickly increase my standard of playing. It became my respite from the struggles of life, for when I was playing I was so engaged with the music that I didn't think at all about how unhappy I was.

Strange as it may seem, when I was at school I'd never realised that I was good at music. All my siblings played an instrument, and my older brother had by now finished his studies and was a professional musician. I'd fallen in love with the flute when attending one of his concerts at just five years of age and had decided then that this was what I was going to play. Now, here I was aged fifteen, at music school, working towards Grade Eight and not even realising I was any good!

Within a couple of years after my parents' divorce our family unit had shrunk to just my mother, an older sister, younger brother and me. My mother worked shifts, and I'd got used the idea that no-one at home was interested in me or came to my concerts, so I stopped telling anyone when I had a concert. I just got on with my life and enjoyed playing.

Even though at my new school I made friends very quickly and had a good circle of friends from the music group, when I wasn't playing music I was missing my old school, the teachers, the friends that I'd known for many years, the area I grew up in and the long walks that I used to have in the countryside. To make matters worse I started to have pain and swelling in one of my knees and was diagnosed with chondromalacia, a softening of the under surface of the kneecap and common in active teenage girls. The hospital doctor didn't think I was resting it enough so they put my leg in a full length plaster cast – that was the end of my sport! I remember one day feeling so lonely and devastated that I walked into a police station and asked how old I had to be to leave home. They replied, "Sixteen," and I said, "I'll stick it out!" then walked out. It was remarkable that no-one asked me anything, but those were the days before child helplines.

A few months later, now sixteen and still struggling to cope with home life and in particular my mother, I started to allow my thoughts to dwell on leaving home. I had no plan and no money – I just didn't know how to carry on.

Then one weekend I was at a friend's house and my mother phoned. This was not unusual; I wasn't allowed to leave the house without writing down the address and phone number of where I was going, and she always phoned to check up on me and generally complain about something, even if I was only out for a couple of hours as was the case that day. It's such a shame that she was never interested in meeting the families of my friends – they were all good people. It's also such a shame that she didn't know me; all I wanted to do was to pass my exams, go to medical school and become a surgeon. I didn't drink alcohol, take drugs or have sex. My friends were all part of the school music group and we just enjoyed being together.

On this occasion the phone call was worse than usual. She told me that she had contacted the music school and spoken to my flute teacher telling her that I wasn't interested in music and that I was only attending so I could avoid housework. That was a blatant lie. She then told me that they didn't want me back! Whatever inner strength I still had in me flowed away rapidly at that moment and was replaced with a depth of pain and devastation like none I had experienced before. There was nothing left for her to take – or so I thought. All I could say was, "I'm not coming home," and for the first time ever I rudely put the phone down.

I had just enough money on me to get a train to Brighton and that's what I did. I had no plan; my mind was hearing those words over and over: "They don't want you back." I hadn't done anything wrong, and what my mother had told them was a lie. I'd been falsely accused of many things at home over the years so that wasn't new, but this time it was different. This had stolen the one thing left in my life that gave me pleasure and sense of achievement. At that moment I didn't think I had anything to live for, yet thankfully I wasn't suicidal; I couldn't take anymore and I just had to get away.

That afternoon I walked from Brighton to Worthing, about twelve miles along the seafront, watching the waves, sometimes walking across the sand and throwing stones into the sea. Gradually my emotions started to settle and I realised that without any money the best I could do was to sleep rough, but this wasn't a long term strategy. By now it was dark. I wasn't hungry, although I hadn't eaten for many hours, but I was conscious that I needed to look after myself.

As with all the walks I went on when I was unhappy, I gradually found an inner strength that spoke sense to me again. Convinced that my mother would have reported me missing by now (she was always threatening to report me to the police even though I never did anything wrong), I found the police station when I reached Worthing, walked in and said, "I've run away from home and I'm not going back." Then I cried intensely for well over five minutes before I could start to tell them what had happened. They treated me well and I sensed they really believed me. Many years later I discovered that my mother had already been to court once for neglect, and I assume this must have been on the records and perhaps why they believed me. That night I stayed in a children's home, and I remember the next morning seeing a small boy aged two at the home who followed me everywhere and was desperate for affection. I learned then that no matter how bad my life was, there was always someone else worse off. At least I was nearly an adult and could leave home. I agreed to return home that day and I was driven to the railway station, given a ticket and promised that someone would come and see me at home. I'd started the process of leaving home properly.

One of the basic needs we all have is to feel secure. Everybody has experienced moments of insecurity because life and relationships are not perfect, though not everyone will recognise their insecurity. Because it is a basic need that we can't live without, if we're not continually finding our security in our relationship with God, we strive to find it by other means, often by taking control over different aspects of our lives or relationships. We may be the sort of person who likes everything in a particular place or order, or maybe we are always looking for the next challenge, not being content with our achievements. Perhaps we're the sort of person who likes to keep up with the ever-changing fashions, or needs lots of holidays to feel good. Perhaps we like to constantly be helping others while not accepting help for ourselves. There is nothing wrong with helping others, holidays, challenges and working hard, but there is a difference between choosing these things as part of our lifestyle and an inner striving to fulfil our needs.

Closely linked to security is our identity, and it's all too easy to get into the trap of finding our identity in what we do, for example our role as a mother, father or in our job. You can test this out quite easily: ask yourself who you are. If your answer is linked to a role then that is where you find your identity.

Some teachings suggest that to satisfy our basic needs of feeling accepted and secure we must strive to improve ourselves and keep achieving; this encourages people to focus on what they think they must achieve rather than on who they are and their value as a person. The problem with this approach is that if one doesn't fulfil what they set out to achieve, there can be a sense of failure, leading to a feeling of unacceptance and a lowering of self-worth. This in turn can lead to further striving or alternatively a continual sense of never coming up to the mark. It's not hard to get into a cycle of needing to continually achieve in order to maintain a sense of worth and acceptance and to base our security on what others think of us in relation to our achievements.

In contrast to this, I've found that if we live life based on what God says about us and find our identity in who we are as children of God, then from this position of acceptance and being secure with God as our Father we can move forward with a good self-esteem and achieve. This achievement is not reliant upon striving; rather it is a natural progression from a fulfilled being. Achievement doesn't need to be big and seen by everyone. To be obedient to what God is asking of you is an achievement and a success. The titles and positions we hold, the medals and certificates we win, and the recognition we receive from others is good, but it is not what will last for eternity. In contrast, storing treasures in heaven will count; giving sacrificially, encouraging and helping others, creating an atmosphere of love and healing are all treasures that will last for ever.

Frank Lake describes the difference between achieving to be accepted and achieving out of acceptance in his Dynamic Cycle, suggesting they are opposite ways to journey through life. The most natural way is to achieve to be accepted – the more we achieve the more we feel significant and because of our significance we feel secure and accepted. The second way, which is God's original plan for us, is to know our security from our place in God's family, from there to realise how significant we are, and then achievement will be a natural progression from our position of wellbeing.

I've found that living from a position of "I'm accepted whether I achieve or not" rather than striving for recognition is far more fulfilling and less stressful. That is not to say I'm perfect – far from it! – we all have our natural self that gets in the way, and I sometimes find myself going about life the opposite direction to God's intended way. I've learned that if I'm feeling under pressure I need to step back and ask myself which way am I travelling; the chances are that at those times I will be travelling round the cycle the wrong way, trying to achieve in order to be accepted, and I'll need to readjust, reminding myself of who I am in God and my value with Him as my Father. The wonderful thing is that when we take time out and stop racing ahead it only takes a moment to realise which way to go and to get back on track.

For Further Reflection

Exodus 23:20
See, I am sending an angel ahead of you to guard you along the way and to bring you to the place I have prepared.

Psalm 37:24
Though we stumble we will not fall for the Lord upholds him with His hand.

Philippians 4:8
Whatever is true, whatever is noble, whatever is right, whatever is pure, whatever is lovely, whatever is admirable, if anything is excellent or praiseworthy, think about such things.

Chapter Ten

The Dream Stealer

With the help of a social worker, my mother agreed that I could leave home at sixteen. I thought I'd have to give up my hopes of becoming a surgeon and knew it was a sacrifice I had to accept. As soon as my O-level exams were over I moved away from the area. The social worker found me a place to stay in a home for people readjusting back to normal life after time in a mental health unit. It wasn't too strange; the people were nice, most of them getting over a nervous breakdown and just needing help. Sometimes I'd sit with them for ages listening to their stories and encouraging them. I wasn't mentally ill, but I'd lost everything so I guess I could empathise with them. My total possessions consisted of one bag of clothes and my flute, a treasured possession that my flute teacher had bought me after my last lesson at music school. (I did go back to the music school after running away to Brighton. My flute teacher said that I couldn't play like I did unless it was from the heart and she wanted me to go on and become a musician; she knew my mother was lying about me.)

I managed to get a cleaning job in a pub to earn a bit of cash. I was told I didn't need to pay for staying at the home, and the social worker said I could start my A-levels at college and they would organise a grant for me. I could stay at the home until I'd finished my studies.

After working through the summer holidays I started at college and was so happy. I loved studying Pure Maths, Chemistry and Biology and was excited that I could still be a surgeon. Life was easy now without the constant pressures of home life, though I continued to have long walks, not because I needed to cool off and restore a calmness inside but because I just loved seeing the trees, sky and beautiful things; they inspired me.

Then one cold, frosty winter morning, just before I was leaving for college, the post arrived and there was a letter for me. I wasn't expecting anything and I opened it with curiosity. I couldn't believe what I read: it was from the social worker saying that I would have to leave college and the home as they couldn't secure me a grant! The reason was that my mother wouldn't agree to sign the forms. I was furious and devastated all at the same time. Why hadn't they told me at the beginning that it was dependent on my mother? I could have told them she wouldn't agree to anything. Instead they'd led me along the path of my dreams and I'd believed them. This time I really *had* lost everything – there was nothing left that could be taken.

I walked around a local park for two hours until I was so cold I had to go back to the home. They were surprised to see me, thinking I was at college. Unable to talk or even cry, I handed them the letter to read and then sat in stunned silence in front of the open fire, drinking hot chocolate until I was warm. I never did step inside the college again or say goodbye to anyone. Several weeks later I received a letter from my Maths teacher saying that they were missing me and that she had every confidence I would succeed in whatever I did. Those words – "I know you will succeed in whatever you do" – have stayed with me and provided strength many times during my life.

How my life turned around from such devastation is nothing short of a miracle and a testimony of how the grace and favour of God works in our lives even when we don't know Him. My belief is that someone was praying for me – maybe one of my teachers – and I say this as an encouragement to you to continue praying for people even when you don't see the answers.

I found a job as a trainee dental nurse and shared a flat. Just over a year later I started training as a general registered nurse and moved into a nurse's home. I made many new friends and had a great time. I never did become a surgeon, though I did think about studying again for this when I was in my early thirties. By then I had a young family and knew if I chose this career my family would have to come second, so I accepted that this was one dream that although I was capable of, wouldn't ever be fulfilled – and I was at peace with that. You see, I'd learned that my identity wasn't about what I could do or what my role was. My identity had to come from who I was, how God had made me unique and the gifting and personality He'd put inside me. I'd discovered that whatever I did, as I walked with God I could be completely me and completely content. I didn't need to strive.

Many years later, after my children had grown up and I was free to do whatever I chose, as I considered my future, my desires and what I wanted to offer back to God, I was surprised to find that it was hard to write down any goals. It was as though I was numb and just couldn't think of any. As I reflected on the reason for this I became aware of the impact that losing my dream of being a surgeon was still having on me. Beginning to get annoyed that something so long ago was still affecting me I had to find a way through so I started to consider what dreams I used to have.

Somehow thinking in terms of dreams was easier than having goals, maybe because dreams are safe in my mind whereas goals are much more tangible and possibly unachievable. One evening I set myself a task of writing a list of a hundred of my dreams, however long ago they were, and within minutes I'd reached ninety-five without much effort. The next step was to take a few of the most important ones and start to consider them as goals that I wanted to achieve. Gradually over time I was able not only to write goals and plans to achieve them, but also to speak openly and share them with others. This was a big step forward as, inwardly and without knowing it, I'd been harbouring a fear that if I said what my goals were someone would snatch them away.

We are all built with dreams and desires inside us. When we're children we have lots. Gradually as we grow older they become less as our experiences in life or negative comments spoken over us erode our desires and passions. When God made us He put inside each one of us the passions and desires that we need to fulfil our dreams and goals in life and to reach our God-given destiny.

Think back to when you were a child. What did you like doing? This is a clue to what you naturally have inside you. Make a list of a hundred of your dreams, let your childlike imagination take the lead and don't hold back. Then take two or three of them and start to consider how they can become your goals and what you need to do to achieve them. Be guided by what God has called you to do. There is nothing wrong with Christians having personal dreams and desires; indeed we are instructed to "write down the revelation/vision" (Habakkuk 2:2). The more you declare what you are going to do, the more likely it will be achieved. It is the enemy, the devil, who wants to keep you quiet and confused. Don't give him any opportunity to hold you back, for God delights in you and He has equipped you to fulfil your God-given passions and desires.

The good news is that dreams can be rekindled, our passions and desires can be re-ignited, and it's never too late to have goals that are achievable. Don't ever let people or circumstances get in the way of what you want to achieve and what God wants to achieve through you.

Romans 8:31
If God is for us who can be against us?

For Further Reflection

Jeremiah 29:11
For I know the plans I have for you, declares the Lord, plans to prosper you and not to harm you, plans to give you hope and a future.

Psalm 32:8
I will instruct you and teach you in the way you should go; I will counsel you and watch over you.

Isaiah 54:10
Though the mountains be shaken and the hills be removed, yet my unfailing love for you will not be shaken ... says the Lord, who has compassion on you.

Chapter Eleven

Reunited

After my parents' divorce I still saw my dad but only from a distance. He was a pharmacist and at that time was working in a chemist located on the small local shopping parade close to my primary school. Each afternoon after school I had to walk past the chemist on my way home. I always looked to see if he was there, but not obviously as I didn't want anyone to notice me looking. My mother had told me that my dad didn't love me anymore and I would be locked up by the police if I spoke to him! When you are young you believe what you are told. I so much wanted to go into the chemist and tell him everything that I was doing at school, show him my new teeth and the gaps where my baby teeth had fallen out and play him the National Anthem on my new recorder without looking at the music; I wanted him to be proud of me.

My Dad had tried having access to us but without success. My younger brother, one of my sisters and I were interviewed all together by a social worker regarding this, and I remember being very frightened at the time. I wanted to see my dad but was too scared to say so in front of the others, having been bullied into keeping quiet by my mother and older brother. I started to dream regularly each night and it was always the same dream; I dreamt my dad was coming back for me, and as he approached the front door I'd see in my dream the police running up the road and I'd wake in a cold sweat.

As I approached teenage years the dreams stopped and I had accepted that I would never have a dad again, even though I knew he was living less than two miles away. After a few years I heard that my dad had married a lady who had two children, one of them a girl. Dreaming at night started again; this time the dream was different. I dreamt I was playing a netball match against another school and my dad was watching. He didn't recognise me and was cheering this other girl who was playing in the opposing team. I used to wake up shaking and saying over and over in my mind, "He's *my* dad, not yours," and feeling very angry.

I never forgot my dad, and many years later, as it was approaching his birthday, I decided to send him a birthday card and write to him. I found his address in the phone book – he hadn't moved since he'd married. Why had I waited so long before contacting him? I still felt guilty that I had not had the courage as a child to stand out against my brother and mother and say that I did want to see him. In addition, I didn't want to be demanding and selfish; he'd made a new life and I was genuinely happy for him. From my childhood memory I knew him; now I wanted to know him from an adult perspective, and I knew this was an opportunity to grasp before it was too late. It had occurred to me that living with regret about a missed opportunity was not a good idea. I sent the birthday card and letter, and the next evening he phoned me. In a way it was strange hearing his voice; I could remember what he looked like but it hadn't occurred to me that I'd forgotten his voice. Now, the more we spoke, the more I recognised his calm, gentle voice that was loving and reassuring.

We arranged a day for him to visit us. It had been thirty-one years since we'd been together, and the first thing I noticed was that I had the same colour eyes as my dad. I felt very special. Later that day after dinner, as we embraced, he said, "I'll never leave you again," and I knew he meant it. In that moment of embrace something quite remarkable happened, I had a deep spiritual encounter of God's fatherly love and that He too would never leave me, and my previous limitations in experiencing God's love just melted away. I realise I was very privileged to be reunited with my dad; so many people don't have this and I can't explain why God allowed this for me – He just did.

It would be lovely to say that all was well after that, but unfortunately my dad was not a strong person. Both my mother and his second wife were controlling women. His wife didn't want us to be part of their life, so most of our relating after that was through letters and phone conversations, even though we lived less than fifteen miles apart.

In the next fourteen years I saw my dad five times. The last two occasions were during his final days in hospital before dying. He wasn't obviously conscious but I could tell from his body language that he knew I was there.

The funeral was interesting. I'd met my half-brother for the first time at the hospital and we instantly got on. Now I would actually meet the girl that had grown up with my dad. I was calm. It wasn't her fault, she didn't owe me anything, and in fact *nobody* owed me anything. I cannot overemphasise the importance of forgiveness and of not retaining resentment or bitterness. Had I done so, the day of the funeral would have been so different and possibly very unpleasant. Despite all that had happened in my life, I still had my own personal memories of my dad. They had been kept safe for many years in my heart and no-one could take them away. You see, I'd already accepted the loss of my dad twice: once as a child; and again after being reunited, when it became clear I couldn't have close contact with him. Now at the funeral, against all natural and logical explanation, I actually felt sorry for my dad's family who were facing their loss for the first time. I felt a love for them that I believe was from God's heart.

God has an amazing way of blessing us when we least expect it. As I travelled home from the funeral, this is what I thought: "If my Dad had said to me as a child, 'Tina, there's a little girl whose dad has just died, and I need to go and help her. It will mean I'm away for a long time, but I will come back to you,' I would have said, 'Okay.' I trusted him."

I believe that thought was straight from God's heart, for at that moment an amazing inner strength was released in me. God blessed me *after* I'd been obedient to Him, loving others in spite of my own grief.

Our loss and how we perceive it is all about perspective. You see, deep down I think I always knew my dad loved me and I also knew he cared about people. In that way we are very similar, so I know that part of him still lives on in me. But I've learned in life that whatever our experience or relationship with our human fathers, the most important thing is that God is my perfect Father and that's all I need.

Relating to God as a Father is not without challenges. All of us have had a human father that wasn't perfect. No parents are perfect, and if we are parents then we will know we aren't perfect either. The challenge is that how we experience and view our human fathers will be transferred to how we experience and view God as our Father.

We're not stuck though, and I've discovered in life that whatever I didn't have during my early developmental years, I can experience and accept through other channels, as God provides. What I mean is that God provides what we need through our relationships, not just through our parents. That's why it's so important not to choose to be independent and avoid people even if it can at times feel easier.

For example, one of our basic needs is positive affirmation. I clearly had a short supply of this as I grew up; the little I had was from my dad initially and then from my teachers. However, throughout my life I've encountered people who have been affirming, and I receive this with gratitude. It's like having radar that spots what I'm lacking, similar to placing pieces of jigsaw into the bigger picture, and then I give thanks to God for providing. Thanking God and being grateful is all part of the healing process and keeps us away from trying to live independently outside of a relationship with Him.

The more grateful I am, the closer I feel to God and the more I experience His fatherly love in a personal way. I've learned that taking time each day to be focused on Him builds my relationship with Him. It's like that in any relationship: if you want to stay friends you have to spend time with each other. When I say 'spend time with Him' I don't mean legalistically reading the Bible, though obviously reading the Bible is important as it is God's word speaking to us. What I mean is to stop everything and just be still in His presence, not asking for anything but telling Him what you're grateful for, then being silent and waiting. This waiting is not about waiting for a reward; it's about sacrificing yourself at His altar. Sometimes the waiting can go on for a long time; sometimes I feel God physically, sometimes I don't. That's not the most important thing. The act of giving myself to Him is more important. As you do this regularly, you'll start to know the closeness of your heavenly Father, your Daddy in Heaven, as He embraces you.

Gradually I've learned to recognise when I'm close to my heavenly Father and when I've run ahead on my own, with my own plans and desires, usually fuelled by excitement and adventure. I don't always get it right but God is the perfect Father; He understands and will guide me back to the right path.

What I've discovered is that in addition to hearing Him speak to me in my inner spirit, I can actually physically feel Him holding me. The first time this happened I was in a chair relaxing and had an overwhelming feeling of sitting on God with His warm arms around me while wrapped in a big, white, soft, fluffy towel. I can't say how long I stayed like this, not wanting or even able to move and just enjoying His love. I was not alone in the room at the time, and those around me probably thought I was asleep.

This experience of God holding me has happened many times since, not with the fluffy towel but the feeling of His arms around me, sometimes when I least expect it. More and more my love for God has increased, with the result that I have become more grateful with a greater desire to be obedient to His word. As I said at the beginning of this book, being a Christian isn't about following a set of rules; it's about a loving relationship with the creator of the universe – awesome!

For Further Reflection

Ezekiel 36:26
I will give you a new heart and put a new spirit in you; I will remove from you your heart of stone ad give you a heart of flesh.

Proverbs 3:5-6
Trust in the Lord with all your heart and lean not on your own understanding; In all your ways acknowledge Him and He will make your paths straight.

1 Peter 5:7
Cast all your anxiety on Him because He cares for you.

John 16:20
You will grieve but your grief will turn to joy.

Chapter Twelve

Living in Freedom

John 8:32
You will know the Truth and the Truth will set you free.

My whole adult life has been about overcoming the obstacles that were preventing me knowing God in an intimate way and pursuing my God-given purpose and destiny. We all have stories, and we all have challenges that get in the way. The good news is that whatever our situation is or has been, we can all be overcomers; don't let anyone or anything cause you to give up hope.

Everyone has suffered disappointments and hurts in their lives. Just like needing a surgical operation to put things right, there will be times when God needs to root out painful thorns that have penetrated our hearts, in order for us to receive love and healing. It may take courage to face personal issues, but remember with your heavenly Father you're never alone.

The more I experienced release and healing, the more able I was to help others find their healing. Living in freedom means that I'm no longer controlled by old patterns of relating and self-protecting; I'm free to be myself without guilt, shame or fear. I believe the key to overcoming is already built within us: it's our choice whether to forgive, control our anger, believe what God says about us and live from a place of acceptance and security, taking spiritual authority over our circumstances. The devil can't steal our key so he tries to hide it from us by keeping us focused on our problems. We need to get our focus back on solutions and move forwards, helping others at the same time.

So why have I left it this long before telling my story? Why wait until my parents have passed away before speaking out? The more God healed me the more I realised that one day I'd share my story more widely so everyone can know the amazing healing and restoring power of a compassionate, loving Father in heaven. This book is not about revenge or resentment against my parents. Far from it; I learned to honour both my mother and father and to love them unconditionally. I believe that neither of them knew the hurt and deprivation I experienced, and I didn't want to risk causing hurt to them by writing this in their lifetime.

In addition I've deliberately not mentioned names or places, in order to protect my siblings.

They all have their own stories that they may or may not choose to share, and for now that remains confidential. My hope is not that you remember my story, but rather that you remember that your Father in heaven is interested in you and wants to walk closely with you. His love for us is so great that He's keen to heal and restore and He provides for us even when we don't know Him.

When I was young I found that going on long walks each time I was upset helped me restore a sense of calmness to my soul. I didn't know God at the time; I wasn't a Christian, I didn't read the Bible and I wasn't religious. After I became a Christian I realised that the voice that had spoken to me during those walks, the voice that I thought was my own inner self, was the same as God's voice. He'd been with me all the time, guiding and directing me, keeping me safe. Whether you believe in God or not, I know He is there with you too.

Once I was a person trapped in my painful circumstances and experiences. I was quiet – exceptionally quiet and withdrawn, as my school reports confirm – and I often didn't know how to express my needs or ask for help. I felt unlovable and a failure, even when I had lots of good friends and was achieving, and I could feel lonely in a crowded room. My self-esteem was low, and I lived out of a sense of guilt rather than knowing my worth as a person created and loved by Father God.

It was not only the lack of love from my parents that left a lasting impact. The constant bullying from my older brother was intolerable to the point that between the ages of twelve and thirteen, when he returned from college at the end of each term, I accepted sexual abuse rather than bullying. I found it was easier to please him than to fight him.

My life now is so different. For me, living in freedom means that I won't be bullied or threatened by anyone or live in fear of anyone. I don't have to abide by manmade rules and regulations (apart from obeying the law of the country) or be swayed by peer pressure. I can make choices about what I do, who I speak to and how I spend my God-given time without feeling threatened. Past circumstances and hurts will not hold me back, and I'm free to live life with God directing me, not by the latest fashion or research, and definitely not by what others would think. I admit that since God has released me I'm far more talkative than ever and probably much more open with my feelings than the average person. I'm not offended when my friends say I'm talking too much – I smile and chuckle inside because it reminds me of how far I've come and all that God has done for me.

I will always choose forgiveness no matter how painful the event, knowing that my heavenly Father will remove every hurt that I experience. I'm not perfect – my friends and family can tell you that –

but I'm content and live at peace with myself and, as far as I am able, with everyone else. I'm a work in progress, but Daddy in Heaven is with me and will continue to be with me for eternity. I'm a special person because God made me, but I'm not more special than you or anybody else. What God has done for me, He will also do for you.

For Further Reflection

Isaiah 41:18
I will make rivers flow
 on barren heights,
And springs within the valleys.
I will turn the desert into pools of water,
And the parched ground into springs.

Recommended Reading

Bill Johnson	When Heaven Invades Earth
R T Kendall	Total Forgiveness
Frank Lake	Clinical Theology
Andy & Janine Mason	Dream Culture
Leanne Payne	The Healing Presence
Derek Prince	Blessing or Curse: You Can Choose
Derek Prince	Entering the Presence of God
Barbara Shleman Ryan	Healing the Hidden Self
David Seamands	Healing for Damaged Emotions
Mark Stibbe	I am your Father

Also from the Publisher

Restoring our Hearts
Paul Collett

We pray to "Our Father in heaven". But many of us have had a disappointing experience of fatherhood; we have not known a good and intimate father.

In this helpful and penetrating book, Paul Collett shows some of the ways God has enabled him to overcome his own wounds and hurts. He also demonstrates that the future revival of the church will be linked to a restoration of the true meaning of fatherhood.

This is a vital book in our day – easy to read yet with depth of understanding.

onwardsandupwards.org/products/restoring-our-hearts